HEALTHY MEXICAN COOKING:

AUTHENTIC LOW-FAT RECIPES

BY VELDA DE LA GARZA, MS, RD

First Edition

APPLETREE PRESS, INC.

Mankato, Minnesota

Appletree Press, Inc.
151 Good Counsel Drive Suite 125
Mankato, MN 56001
Phone: (507) 345-4848
FAX: (507) 345-3002
Website: www.appletree-press.com

Cataloging-in-Publication Data
de la Garza, Velda.
Healthy Mexican Cooking: authentic low-fat recipes / Velda de la Garza ; editors,
Linda J. Hachfeld and Faith E. W. Winchester. Mankato, MN : Appletree Press, c 1995.
256 p. : col. ill. ; 23 cm.
Includes index.
Summary: Healthy Mexican Cooking enables readers to prepare authentic, traditional
Mexican food with few ingredients, practical preparation times and moderate to low calories.
This book contains over 160 low-fat, heart-healthy recipes, each with nutritional analysis
and diabetic exchanges. Includes special sections on the nutrition label (in Spanish and
English), tools and ingredients for the Mexican kitchen, glossary of Hispanic food and
ingredient terms and specialty supplier list.
ISBN 0-9620471-5-5
1. Cookery, Mexican. 2. Low-fat diet—Recipes. 3.Diabetes—Diet therapy
—Recipes. 4. Diabetes—Nutritional aspects. I. Title. II. Hachfeld, Linda, J.
III. Winchester, Faith E. W.
TX716   95-80011
641.5972   CIP

First Edition, first – third printing: 19,000 copies

Acknowledgements: First Printing Cover Design by Villager Graphics
                   Second Printing Cover Design by Kath Christensen Graphic Design

Recipes featured on the Front and Back Cover: *Pinto Bean Salad*, page 126
                                               Mushroom Enchiladas, page 134

Editors: Linda Hachfeld and Faith Winchester
Assistant: Johnna Solting

Third Printing Cover Design: Timothy Halldin, Pike Graphics
Food Photography, Front and Back Cover: Beatriz Da Costa
Food & Prop Styling, Front and Back Cover: Roscoe Betsill and Helen Crowther
Artwork by Kate Thomssen

ABOUT THE AUTHOR

Velda de la Garza is a Registered Dietitian residing in McAllen, Texas. Being Hispanic, she has first hand knowledge of typical Mexican foods. Velda received her Bachelor's degree in Nutrition from the University of Texas at Austin and completed a dietetic internship at St. Mary's Hospital affiliated with the Mayo Clinic in Rochester, Minnesota. She was granted a Master's of Science degree in Nutrition from Texas Woman's University.

Velda now teaches classes in heart healthy eating. She has also been lecturer/instructor at The University of Texas-Pan American. Her previous experience as a dietitian has been at numerous hospitals including M.D. Anderson Hospital in Houston. She also has worked as a consultant for the University of Texas Health Science Center in Houston and as a Renal Dietitian Specialist. She is the busy mother of three children, Christina, Jorge and Laura. Her husband, Jorge, is a cardiothoracic surgeon in private practice.

Even as a young girl, Velda enjoyed cooking for her family and learning about traditional foods from her grandmother, great aunts, mother and father. Using her knowledge of nutrition in combination with her love of cooking, she has compiled healthy versions of these much loved Mexican foods. With the current interest in healthier living, many will enjoy this wonderful collection of healthy Mexican foods.

THIS BOOK IS DEDICATED TO:

My husband Jorge, for his love and support

My children Christina, Jorge and Laura, for their testing and help

My parents, for their encouragement to achieve wonderful things

My parents-in-law, for their many words of encouragement

My dear friend Ellen

TABLE OF CONTENTS

INTRODUCTION

Food is such an important part of Hispanic culture. We use food to celebrate the important stages of our lives. From baptisms to weddings to wakes, food forms the glue of life that brings us together and binds us as families and friends. Even our Aztec ancestors were known to have prepared tamales using wild game in the 1500's. Many deep-rooted traditions go along with that ever so satisfying food that represents our Spanish, Indian and Mexican heritage.

Most of this book's recipes are the type I enjoy preparing — not too many ingredients, nor too long a preparation period and not too high in calories. Many recipes are the ones I learned to cook at home with my mother; some are from my husband's family. Although the ingredients have changed somewhat, the food is still representative of hundreds of years of history and culture. These foods maintain their tradition in our families, despite borders, economics and the passing of time. Also reflected in my collection are the recipes I collected while living in different parts of the country. Hispanics throughout the Southwest use the same basic ingredients with different flavorful preparations.

The recipes and guidelines in this book offer a healthy alternative to the rich foods many Hispanics are accustomed to eating. While Mexican food can be heaven for the palate, more often than not it is rich in calories, cholesterol and saturated fats.

Unfortunately, far too many Hispanics are prone to diet-related diseases such as obesity, diabetes and heart disease. Recent surveys have shown that the typical Hispanic diet is high in animal fat and refined sugar and deficient in fresh fruits and vegetables.

The most recent National Health and Nutrition Examination Survey showed that nearly 47% of Hispanic women were overweight (Kuczmarski 205). Interpreting this data can mean than almost half the female Hispanic population is at greater risk for developing diet-related diseases such as diabetes and heart disease.

Simultaneously, overwhelming research is telling us it is wiser to consume a diet lower in animal fat, total fat and sugar. We are being advised by health specialists to consume more fruits and vegetables to help prevent certain types of cancer and other diseases. It is believed that about 35% of all cancers may be related to diet (Smolin 152).

Adapting to a healthier diet is not painful, and often, the steps include becoming more conscious of the foods purchased at the grocery store, knowing how to prepare these foods for the family at home, and being mindful of how much is eaten. Should a person choose to eat out, it is important to know how to select healthier restaurant foods.

This cookbook has been prepared to show that many of these steps can be taken with relative ease. Most traditional foods can be modified to be healthier while retaining much of their wonderful flavor. In most recipes, the amounts of seasonings and vegetables have been increased to add flavor without too many additional calories.

Included in this collection are many recipes to show all those interested in Mexican foods that satisfaction does not have to be a plate full of fried food oozing orange grease. The recipes in HEALTHY MEXICAN COOKING are delicious and healthy!

Every one of us enjoys going out to eat for the pleasure of being served good food. Many restaurants offer foods rich in flavor and fat. Fast food restaurants in particular, are known to offer foods very high in fat and low in vitamins and other nutrients (Whitney 472). Occasionally, eating out fits into a healthy eating plan if you've learned to make wise decisions about the food you select to eat.

But it is important to know that by preparing food at home, you control what goes into food preparation and how much goes onto the plate. Being knowledgeable about healthy food preparation will help a person prepare and eat healthier foods at home.

Although not specifically for diabetes, these recipes, except for some desserts, are within guidelines for diabetics. Some of the recipes can be further modified with the use of sugar substitute. Most of the foods are moderate in sodium following general guidelines for good health. If your physician has recommended decreasing salt for medical reasons, many of the recipes can be further adapted using low-sodium products.

Reducing fats in the diet, especially saturated fats, and including more fruits, vegetables and fiber will help you lead a healthier life. If your family is at risk for certain types of diseases related to diet, it is vital to adapt to a healthier lifestyle, including making some diet changes. Traditional foods can still be eaten, but new steps in preparing them should be used. It is simply not true that everything worth eating is sinful or fattening.

There is a great deal of research showing the importance of good nutrition in the prevention of many diseases. Healthy foods pack powerful nutrients that will promote health. As the saying goes in Spanish —

"Que tus alimentos seyan tus medicinas."
May healthy foods be your foundation for a healthy life.

Works Cited

Kuczmarski, R. "Increasing Prevalence of Overweight Among United States Adults." Journal of the American Medical Association. 20 July 1994: 205.

Smolin, Lori and Mary Grosvenor. NUTRITION SCIENCE AND APPLICATIONS. Fort Worth: Saunders College Publishing, 1994.

Whitney, Eleanor, Corrine Caldo and Sharon Rolfes. UNDERSTANDING NORMAL AND CLINICAL NUTRITION. St. Paul: West Publishing Company, 1991.

SPECIAL THANKS TO CONTRIBUTORS:

Gonzalo Garza
Aida Garza
Kika de la Garza
Lucille de la Garza
Isabel Hinojosa
Maria Z. Garza
Ellen Crouse
Linda Trevino, RD
Frances Garza, RN
Stella Garza, RN
Dolores Gutierrez
Nena Bedoya
Lupita Garza
Delia Garza
Leonor Garza
Elida Garza
Vela Family
Ruth Alpert
Lucille Barrera
Edna Ramon, RD
Irma Trigo
Martha Valerio
Elizabeth Pena
Margarita Gutierrez
Kathy Morin, R.N.
Maria Garza
Nena M. Garza, RD

SPECIAL THANKS FOR TECHNICAL SUPPORT:

Lenore Frydrychowicz, M.S., R.D.
Linda Trevino, R.D.
Mary Sanchez, M.S.,R.D.
Amelia Gorena-Walsh, Ph.D.
Paul Walsh
Ileana Vicinaiz, RD

ANALYSIS PROGRAMS

Recipes were analyzed using the following programs:
Sante (For Good Health) Hopkins Technology. Hopkins, Minnesota, 1991.
Nutritionist III. N-Squared Computing. Salem, Oregon, 1989.

CHAPTER ONE

CHAPTER ONE

HEART DISEASE

Almost half of all deaths annually in the United States are caused by heart attacks. Heart disease is the leading cause of death in our country. Cost for treatment of heart disease approaches about ninety billion dollars per year. About one in two Americans will die of cardiovascular disease, one every thirty-four seconds (AHA 1).

Heart attacks occur when arteries become completely blocked or a blood clot forms in a clogged artery and stops the flow of blood to the heart. The heart, a muscle, will become damaged due to the lack of blood and oxygen provided by the blood.

Atherosclerosis, or "hardening of the arteries," is due partially to a high level of cholesterol and triglycerides in the blood. Atherosclerosis is the leading contributor to many heart attack and stroke deaths (AHA 8).

In the Hispanic population, cigarette smoking, obesity and a high-fat diet are all factors contributing to heart disease. One-third of all deaths in Hispanics is related to diseases of the heart and cerebrovascular disease.

There are many complex factors that contribute to the development of atherosclerosis. These include heredity, sex and age. Heart attacks appear to be more prevalent in some families and are more common in men. Advancing age increases chances for cardiovascular disease problems for both men and women.

Although heart disease is perceived as a "man's problem," it strikes women, too, only 6-10 years later than men. According to William Castelli, director of the Framingham Heart Study, "Once past menopause, women develop coronary heart disease at the same rate as men," (Women and Heart Disease). Heredity, sex and age are factors that cannot be controlled.

Other factors also appear to contribute to the development of heart disease and can be controlled. Smoking, being overweight, having high blood pressure, high blood cholesterol, diabetes, and not exercising are proven risk factors for cardiovascular diseases.

Smoking is the single greatest preventable cause of death. Smoking strains the heart because it makes the blood vessels constrict. It also causes temporary changes in the heart, making it beat faster and raising blood pressure. In addition, smoking increases the level of carbon monoxide in the blood, decreasing the amount of oxygen available to the heart (AHA 29).

High blood pressure, also known as hypertension, is a major risk factor for heart disease and is the most important risk factor for stroke. Even slightly high levels double the risk. High blood pressure is sometimes called the "silent killer" because most people have it without feeling sick. Therefore, it's important to have blood pressure checked each time you see your physician or other health professional.

Further discussion of diabetes, obesity, exercise and prevention of heart disease follow. It is important to have regular checkups, exercise, eat a healthy diet, maintain a healthy body weight and not smoke to reduce the risk of heart disease.

DIABETES

Mexican-American adults have almost two to three times the incidence of diabetes than that of Anglo-Americans (Algert 1).

Diabetes is a disease in which the body does not produce or properly use insulin. The sugars and starches consumed are converted by the body into glucose. Glucose is then sent to each cell in the body for immediate use or for storage. Insulin, a hormone produced by the pancreas, is necessary to help transport the glucose into each cell. When insulin cannot enter the cell, an excess of glucose results and "spills" into the urine. This problem causes many other serious problems relating to the metabolism of all nutrients (Whitney 824).

Diabetes, when uncontrolled or left untreated, can lead to many serious complications. These include:

* **Development of atherosclerosis (hardening of the arteries)** can lead to a stroke, heart attack, or amputation of affected limbs. More than 80% of people who have diabetes die of some type of cardiovascular disease, usually heart attack. The risk of death from coronary heart

disease is doubled in women with diabetes. Diabetes is often called a "woman's disease" because after age 45, about twice as many women as men develop diabetes. For unknown reasons, the risks of heart disease and heart-related deaths are higher for diabetic women than for diabetic men (Sandmaier 26).

* **Hardening of small arteries** may damage eyes and kidneys. Both can have serious complications such as blindness and loss of kidney function, which may require dialysis.

* **Nerve and blood vessel damage and high blood pressure** resulting from high blood sugar (Whitney 828).

* **Birth defects** in babies of pregnant women with diabetes (Whitney 844).

Complications and resulting hospitalizations are very costly. According to the American Diabetes Association, costs for diabetes-related care run almost $20 billion annually. Often medical insurance is much higher for a person diagnosed with diabetes.

While there is no cure for diabetes, there are steps one can take to control it. 85% of all noninsulin dependent diabetics are at least 20% overweight, and the risk of developing diabetes doubles for every 20% increase in weight over ideal body weight. Studies have shown that in the obese person with diabetes, weight reduction can lead to more normal blood sugars. In many cases, this means no insulin or other medications for diabetes. The control of diabetes may depend on a lifetime of healthy eating (limiting calories and fat), losing excess body weight and increasing physical activity.

The key word in managing diabetes is *control.* A person with diabetes must be very careful to control his or her blood sugar according to the recommendations of his or her physician. By controlling weight and blood sugar, a person may be able to avert and/or delay some of the problems that are inherent to diabetes. Given the seriousness of these problems, avoiding them seems well worth the effort.

OBESITY

Health professionals often define obesity by first determining a person's healthy body weight. The person that is 20% over that healthy weight is considered obese. A person who is considerably over his or her healthy weight, but not more than 20% over, is classified as overweight. Weight does not tell the health professional how fat a person is, but it is an indicator of being "overfat." The formula that may be used to compute healthy body weight is as follows:

> **Men:** 106 pounds for the first 5 feet in height
> Add 6 pounds for each additional inch
> Example: Male 5 feet 9 inches
> Healthy weight= 160 pounds
>
> **Women:** 100 pounds for the first 5 feet in height
> Add 5 pounds for each additional inch
> Example: Female 5 feet 2 inches
> Healthy weight=110 pounds (Hamwi 74)

Why is obesity harmful?

An obese person is at increased risk of developing many health problems.

Heart disease: People who are 30% overweight are more likely to develop heart- related problems even if they have no other risk factors (NIH 23). The heart of an obese person has to work much harder than that of a nonobese person (Whitney 865). Research also suggests that body shape as well as weight affects heart health. "Apple-shaped" individuals with extra fat at the waistline may have a higher risk than "pear-shaped" people with heavy hips and thighs. If your waist is larger than the size of your hips, you may have a higher risk for coronary heart disease (Sandmaier 25).

Diabetes: Diabetes is a very serious disease in which the body does not produce enough or properly use insulin. The more excess weight a person has, the greater the demands on the body's supply of insulin. Uncontrolled diabetes may lead to stroke, heart attack, blindness and kidney failure, among other medical problems (Whitney 828).

High blood pressure: Greater amounts of fatty tissue increase the burden on the circulatory system. Many persons with high blood pressure have strokes, congestive heart failure and kidney failure (Whitney 865).

Osteoarthritis: In obese persons, symptoms may become worse due to excess pressure on weight-bearing joints such as knees and hips (Whitney 534).

An obese person will have a greater chance of developing gallbladder problems (Whitney 790). A high fat, high cholesterol diet may contribute to gallstones. Eighty percent of gallstones are composed of cholesterol. Also, obese patients have a greater possibility of more serious medical problems after surgery (Berkow 953). These complications include, among others, problems with wound healing and blood clots.

Research indicates that breast, colon and uterine cancers may be related to obesity (ACS 22).

What causes obesity?

Approximately 35% of adult women, 31% of adult men and 25% of children and adolescents in the United States are obese (Food & Nutrition Board 1995). For Mexican-Americans, the numbers increase to 35.5% of men and 46.7% of women who are overweight (Kuczmarski 210).

Recent studies have shown that there is a very strong genetic factor in obesity. If one parent or a close family member is obese, chance are greater that a person will also be obese. If both parents are obese, the chances are even greater still (Whitney 366). These are factors that cannot be changed, but there are factors that can be controlled to limit weight gain and the tendency to become overweight or obese.

Two of these factors include increasing exercise and changing eating habits.

PREVENTION

Healthy Eating Habits

By the time a person has been diagnosed with heart disease, the body has undergone years of changes and injury to the blood vessels. The damage has been done and diet and medication may slow the progressive damage, but rarely will the disease disappear.

Some current promising research shows that perhaps there can be a degree of reversal of artery blockage by following a very strict vegetarian-type diet (Ornish). This concept is undergoing further investigation, but the fact remains that the most effective program against heart disease is prevention.

To prevent heart disease a person must become knowledgeable about the risk factors for heart disease. As explained earlier in the chapter, there are some things a person will not be able to change, but there are more risk factors that a person can control. To help avoid a heart attack or stroke, it is important to be aware of the positive changes that can be made in what we choose to eat and the amount of physical activity in our daily lives.

The health of our hearts has much to do with the food we eat. Changing our eating habits according to the Dietary Guidelines for Americans (see **Chapter 2**) lessens our risk of heart disease in three ways:

* It helps reduce high blood cholesterol.

* It helps control high blood pressure.

* It helps take off extra pounds.

The kinds of eating habits that are good for your heart may also prevent certain types of cancer and a number of other health problems.

High Blood Cholesterol

The higher the blood cholesterol level, the higher the heart disease risk. For all adults, a desirable blood cholesterol level is less than 200 mg/dL. A level of 240 mg/dL or above is considered "high" blood cholesterol, but even levels in the "borderline-high" category (200-239 mg/dL) increases the risk of heart disease. Blood cholesterol levels should be checked once every 5 years (AHA 21).

Total blood cholesterol is the first measurement used to identify persons with high blood cholesterol. A more complete "cholesterol profile" includes measuring LDL- and HDL-cholesterol. LDL-cholesterol carries most of the cholesterol in the blood, thus the higher the LDL number, the higher the risk for coronary heart disease. HDL-cholesterol helps remove cholesterol from the blood, preventing it from piling up in the arteries, thus the higher this number, the lower the risk for coronary heart disease. An LDL level below 130 mg/dL is desirable and an HDL level above 35 is recommended (Whitney 857).

Lowering Blood Cholesterol

One major study showed that each 1 percent of reduction in blood cholesterol produced a 2 percent reduction in the number of heart attacks. This means that if you lower your blood cholesterol by 25 percent, you may cut your risk of heart attack in half (Sandmaier 47).

Controlling your diet is an effective method by which you can lower blood cholesterol to help prevent heart disease. The following are general guidelines for a healthy diet. Before following any special diet, check with a physician.

* Limit consumption of meat, especially red meat. Studies have shown a relationship between consumption of red meats and heart disease. Try to include at least two "meatless" meals every week. When you do eat meat, a three-ounce serving should be your guideline. Three ounces is roughly the size and thickness of the palm of the hand or the size of a deck of cards. A meal of beans combined with corn or rice makes an excellent substitute for meat in the diet.

* Decrease your consumption of cholesterol and saturated fat. All cholesterol comes from animal sources.

Saturated fat in the diet increases cholesterol and other harmful fats in the blood (see **Chapter 2** for sources of saturated fat). Saturated fat comes primarily from animal sources. The "tropical oils" palm and coconut oil are high in saturated fat and should be avoided. These are often found in processed foods such as cookies, crackers and other snack foods.

Polyunsaturated fat in the diet appears to lower blood cholesterol. This type of fat appears to play a most important role in cardiovascular disease and is found in plants and seafood. Corn, sunflower, soybean, and walnut oils are examples of polyunsaturated fats.

Monounsaturated fat in the diet also reduces blood cholesterol. Like polyunsaturated fats, this fat is liquid at room temperature. Olive and canola oils, peanuts and fish are rich in monosaturated fats.

To lessen your chances of getting coronary heart disease, the total fat in your diet should be no more than 30% of the total calories. Saturated fat should make up less than 10% of total calories; polyunsaturated fat should be no more than 10%; monosaturated fat should make up 10-15% of total calories. Keep cholesterol intake at less than 300 mg/day.

* Try to include two servings of "fatty" fish per week in your diet. Recommended fish include red salmon, mackerel, sardines and albacore tuna.

* Decrease total fat in your diet. Fat is a rich source of calories, regardless of the source. Limit all fried and oily foods. Limit desserts made with fats. Even healthier oils add lots of calories to the diet. Learn the fat content of foods commonly eaten.

* Increase amounts of fruits and vegetables. Many studies are showing the importance of fruits and vegetables in disease prevention. Opt for highly-colored vegetables and fruits which are usually richer sources of vitamins and minerals. Spinach, cantaloupe, oranges, strawberries and tomatoes are good examples. Fruits and vegetables are healthiest when eaten uncooked.

* Increase use of whole grains in the diet. Whole grains contain many minerals and other nutrients important to your health. Whole grains such as oatmeal are also good sources of fiber which has been shown to have a cholesterol lowering effect. Whole wheat bread and tortillas, wheat cereals and whole grain cereals are all good whole grain sources.

Eating a healthy diet will require lifetime changes. Changing a diet for a few weeks will not resolve or prevent health problems. Rather, positive changes made for the long term will make a difference in a person's overall health.

EXERCISE

According to the American Heart Association, lack of exercise advances us one step closer to getting heart disease. Lack of exercise has been given equal billing with being overweight, smoking and having a family history of heart disease.

1) Exercise is a challenge to physically condition the body. In the process, a person will feel better, look better, and have better health. Having a conditioned body improves metabolism and strengthens the heart and lungs (Whitney 833).

2) People with adult onset diabetes have shown improvement in blood glucose levels after being on a good exercise program (Whitney 833). Many physicians working with diabetic patients will insist on their patients getting daily exercise.

3) An exercise program is most important to weight control, as exercise has been shown to reduce total body fat. Exercise requires calorie expenditure, aiding any weight loss program. Additionally, a good exercise program will help a person's bones become stronger, and this may decrease to some degree the amount of bone loss in women with osteoporosis (Cooper 7).

4) Exercise also increases the production of the brain's morphine-like compounds, endorphins, giving the physically fit person a feeling of well being (Smolin 390).

Meeting the challenge is very simple. The first step is to decide to make the program a long term commitment, then decide what program fits best. Fitness programs vary from walking around the neighborhood to engaging a personal fitness trainer. While walking costs little or nothing, and a fitness trainer may be more costly, it is most important that a program be designed to be the most workable with an individual schedule. It should be entertaining and varied enough to avoid boredom. It should be done consistently, and it should be a healthy exercise for the person doing it.

One should always check with a doctor before starting any exercise program and get his or her approval to be absolutely sure that the body will withstand the rigors of an exercise program. It is extremely important for a person to check with a doctor before beginning an exercise program if he or she is:

* Taking blood pressure or heart medication

* Experiencing any chest pain or dizzy spells

* Very heavy (more than 20% over healthy body weight)

* Over 65

Get That Heart Pumping!

Most likely the best exercise from many aspects is **walking**. It is basically free, can be done conveniently and can be exhilarating!

It is important, however, to understand that exercise is supposed to strengthen as many muscles in the body as possible, especially the heart muscle. A snail's pace will not do it!

Walking is the best form of exercise for people who are just beginning an exercise program, are very overweight, or are older. There is little chance of injury, but also little gain if not done properly. It costs nothing to enjoy a vigorous walk. One doesn't need a set schedule, and a walk can be an enjoyable way to end a long day. The only equipment needed is a good pair of walking shoes.

Current recommendations for exercise according to the Cooper Clinic are:
Women — 2 miles in less than 30 minutes at least 3 days a week or 2 miles in 30-minutes, 5-6 days a week.

Men — 2 miles in less than 27 minutes at least 3 days a week or 2 miles in 30-40 minutes, 6-7 days a week.

Becoming a member of a health club offers other alternatives for exercising. One of the many benefits of working out at a health club is feeling inspired by working alongside healthy, fit individuals. Additionally, there are many types of equipment that can help to vary the workout and get better overall training. Counselors at fitness centers can offer advice on personal fitness programs and may be able to do a body composition analysis. It is rewarding for some individuals to measure body composition periodically for reinforcement of the benefits of their exercise program.

Another option is to purchase home video **workout tapes**. These are perfect for inclement weather or for those times when a parent is homebound with children. There are many different types and levels available. It might be a good idea to rent one and preview the program to determine if it is interesting as well as challenging.

The numerous early morning fitness programs on cable TV also are great, but one should adjust the workout to his or her own fitness level. Beginners, overweight people and older people may find it necessary to slow them down a bit. People with a higher degree of fitness may need to work with weights to achieve a better workout. The advantages of TV fitness programs include personal privacy and little or no cost.

Biking is still another great way to get exercise and enjoy the outdoors. It is an opportunity for family time that gets everyone involved.

We are fortunate to have many, many forms of exercise available to us. Unfortunately, there are too many stationary bicycles and stair steppers sitting in people's bedrooms and garages unused, reminders of forgotten commitments to "get in shape."

There are a number of other options to help a person vary her exercise program. Buying a good old fashioned jump rope and using it offers still more variety. Jumping rope can be a great aerobic workout.

It is important to vary the exercise program, including three thirty-minute aerobic workouts a week (Cooper 6). Aerobic exercise is one of the most important components of achieving desired weight as well as achieving and maintaining good health.

Some of the **best results of good exercise** include strengthening the heart's ability to pump blood more efficiently, and developing the circulatory system to work at its best, delivering oxygen to all parts of the body (Cooper 7). These, in turn, mean:

☺ Better breathing — stronger chest muscles
☺ Improved stamina — stronger heart and body
☺ More energy — body systems run more efficiently.

The heart is a muscle, and its performance will be enhanced by exercise.

A healthier heart and body will be the result of a solid, long term commitment to health. The payback will be a longer, healthier life — a priceless gift.

Works Cited

Algert, Susan, et al. MEXICAN-AMERICAN FOOD PRACTICES, CUSTOMS AND HOLIDAYS: ETHNIC AND REGIONAL FOOD PRACTICES. American Dietetic Association, American Diabetes Association. Chicago, 1989.

American Heart Association. AYUDE A SU CORAZON. Dallas National Center, 1994.

American Heart Association. 1992 HEART AND STROKE FACTS. Dallas National Center, 1992.

Berkow, Robert and Andrew Fletcher. THE MERCK MANUAL OF DIAGNOSIS AND THERAPY. Rathway: Merck and Company, 1987.

American Cancer Society. CANCER FACTS AND FIGURES 1990. Atlanta, 1990.

Cooper, Kenneth. STEPS FOR LIFE: 12 WAYS FOR INDIVIDUALS TO IMPROVE THE ODDS FOR A LIFETIME OF GOOD HEALTH AND REDUCE THE COST OF HEALTH CARE. Dallas: Cooper Institute for Aerobic Research: 1994.

"Genetics and Nutrition: New Discoveries." DAIRY COUNCIL DIGEST 66/4 (July/August 1995): 19-24.

Hamwi, G.J. "Therapy: Changing Dietary Concepts." DIABETES MELLITUS DIAGNOSIS AND TREATMENT. New York: American Diabetes Association, 1964.

Ornish, Dean. DEAN ORNISH'S PROGRAM FOR REVERSING HEART DISEASE. New York: Random House, 1990.

Sandmaier, Marie. THE HEALTHY HEART HANDBOOK. Washington DC: The National Heart, Lung and Blood Institute, 1992.

Smolin, Lori and Mary Grosvenor. NUTRITION SCIENCE AND APPLICATIONS. Fort Worth: Saunders College Publishing, 1994.

Whitney, Eleanor and Sharon Rolfes. UNDERSTANDING NUTRITION. St. Paul: West Publishing Company, 1993.

The Cooper Institute for Aerobics Research. RESEARCH NEWS: FITNESS AND MORTALITY. Dallas: 1995.

Women & Heart Disease video. American Heart Association, 1989.

CHAPTER TWO

CHAPTER TWO

THE FOOD GUIDE PYRAMID

The United States Department of Agriculture has designed the Food Guide Pyramid based on current scientific recommendations for healthy eating.

While in the past meat was the focus of America's meals, its importance is now lessened, and emphasis is placed on grains and breads as the foundation of the diet, followed by fruits and vegetables.

Because of the many health problems that are related to a high intake of fatty foods, the current recommendation for meat consumption is to eat smaller quantities, placing it higher up on the pyramid. Lowfat milk and lowfat milk products are also important, and they share equal weight with the meat group. Of lesser importance, to be consumed occasionally, are sweets and fatty foods.

The Hispanic diet is typically low in fruits and vegetables and high in simple sugars. The focus of the traditional Mexican-American meal is meat, and the rest of the meal is prepared to complement the main course. Portions are usually large, and meals are typically served family-style.

To adapt to a healthier diet using the Food Guide Pyramid as a guide, the following suggestions are made:

* Make the foundation of your meals grains and cereals. Many low-fat selections are available such as corn tortillas, bolillos, whole grain cereals, brown and white rice, and whole wheat tortillas prepared with oil.

* Eat more fruits and vegetables. Five servings of nutrient-rich fruits and vegetables is desirable. Think color. The richer the color of fruits and vegetables, the higher the nutrient content. Tomato-based salsas are excellent sources of vitamins. Salsas add flavor to the diet while adding minimal calories or sodium. Adding vegetables to rice and beans is a good way to eat more vegetables. Fruits and vegetables are healthiest when eaten without extra fats or sauces, and they add the benefit of increased fiber intake.

* The portion of low-fat meat eaten twice a day should be the size of a deck of cards. Examine a deck of cards. The small size may surprise you. It is that size portion of a low-fat meat that your body requires twice each day. Any amount over that is unnecessary. Meats can be prepared together with rice or pasta dishes to "stretch" the meal and limit the amount of meat eaten. Chicken with rice or beef with vermicelli are good examples. By combining small amounts of meat with grains or pasta, the food dollar goes farther, and the meal is healthier.

* Lowfat milk and milk products are important for every age and are the best sources of calcium in our diets. Calcium is vital to body functions and to the structure of bones. A diet low in calcium during childhood will likely result in weak bones. During the adult years a low intake of calcium can further weaken bones. Osteoporosis is a costly health problem that can be avoided with a good intake of calcium-rich foods. Lowfat cheeses incorporated into foods are also good sources of calcium.

* Limit sugars and fats in your diet. A heart healthy diet eliminates fried and fatty foods. A person should consume no more than 1-3 teaspoons of oils/fats per day (Cooper 8). Sugars add many calories to the diet. If too many sugary and fatty foods are eaten, it is very likely that a person will become overweight. Learn the number of fat grams recommended for your diet. Then count grams of fat in all foods you eat. Look at the sugar content of foods. Every 4 grams of sugar in a food equals one teaspoon of sugar. Some soft drinks contain 12-14 teaspoons of sugar!

The Food Guide Pyramid:
A Guide to Daily Food Choices

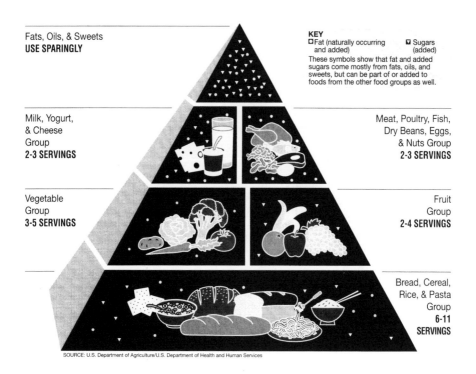

Fats, Oils, & Sweets
USE SPARINGLY

KEY
☐ Fat (naturally occurring and added)   ◪ Sugars (added)
These symbols show that fat and added sugars come mostly from fats, oils, and sweets, but can be part of or added to foods from the other food groups as well.

Milk, Yogurt, & Cheese Group
2-3 SERVINGS

Meat, Poultry, Fish, Dry Beans, Eggs, & Nuts Group
2-3 SERVINGS

Vegetable Group
3-5 SERVINGS

Fruit Group
2-4 SERVINGS

Bread, Cereal, Rice, & Pasta Group
6-11 SERVINGS

SOURCE: U.S. Department of Agriculture/U.S. Department of Health and Human Services

DIETARY GUIDELINES FOR AMERICANS

Use these seven guidelines together as you choose a healthful and enjoyable diet.

* Eat a variety of foods.

* Maintain a healthy weight.

* Choose a diet low in fat, saturated fat and cholesterol.

* Choose a diet with plenty of vegetables, fruits and grain products.

* Use sugars only in moderation.

* Use salt and sodium only in moderation.

* If you drink alcoholic beverages, do so in moderation.

FOOD LABELS

Federal regulations state that all foods must include a standard nutrition label. To the health-conscious consumer, this is extremely important. At a glance, the knowledgeable shopper can tell whether and how a particular food fits into a diet plan.

The new food label has many strong points.

* Realistic serving portions for that particular food.

* Percentage of a "Daily Value" for a particular nutrient based on a 2,000 calorie diet. So, when reading a label, you may see a product has only 5 grams of saturated fat, which sounds low, but in reality is 25% of the total Daily Value of saturated fat for a 2,000 calorie diet.

* Values for the nutrients more important to today's health-conscious consumer such as fat, saturated fat, cholesterol, sodium and calories.

Some practical guidelines for using the nutrition label include:

* Know approximately how many calories per day you require. A Registered Dietitian can help determine your calorie needs. Knowing how many calories you require will help you adjust the values listed on the label to meet your particular needs. For example, a woman who needs 1500 calories per day will require lesser amounts of nutrients listed. Therefore 25% of the Daily Value may actually be 30% for a person consuming less than 2,000 a day. If this is the case, consume a smaller portion of the food or avoid the food.

* Identify serving portions carefully. Is the serving size listed a truly realistic portion? A good example is ice cream, often listed in one half cup portions. Measure one half cup of ice cream. Even though one half cup has only 6 grams of fat, one and a half cups, perhaps a more realistic serving, will have three times that much or 18 grams, making that "low-fat" food into a high-fat food.

* A rough rule of thumb: If the food has more than 20% Daily Value for both fat and saturated fat, it is wiser to make another choice. Remember, this number is based on an intake of 2,000 calories and 65 grams of fat. A person may need fewer calories and therefore fewer grams of fat.

* Evaluate the size of the food. Some individually packaged foods are made in very small sizes. The small size may not be filling and may prompt a person to eat more than one serving.

* A "low" cholesterol food has 20 mg cholesterol. Use this number as a guide (Smolin 156). Recommended intake for cholesterol is less than 300 mg per day. An egg yolk has 213 mg cholesterol, and is one of the highest cholesterol foods. Limit egg yolks to four a week. Egg white is cholesterol-free.

*   A low-fat food means a healthier food, sometimes. Today's consumer wants low-fat foods. Many food companies have responded to this need by producing lower fat foods, but have in turn increased the sugar in some products or make portions smaller. Read the label carefully. Try to eat low-fat and low-calorie foods.

*   For a person with heart problems or one following a low-sodium diet for high blood pressure, the amount of sodium eaten per day should be no more than 2,000 mg. Check with your physician. For the average person, the amount should be 3,000 mg. Keep these numbers in mind when reading food labels. Many companies have reduced-sodium foods.

Work Cited

Cooper, Kenneth. STEPS FOR LIFE: 12 WAYS FOR INDIVIDUALS TO IMPROVE THE ODDS FOR A LIFETIME OF GOOD HEALTH AND REDUCE THE COST OF HEALTH CARE. Dallas: Cooper Institute for Aerobic Research, 1994.

Serving Size

Is your serving the same size as the one on the label? If you eat double the serving size listed, you need to double the nutrient and calorie values. If you eat one-half the serving size shown here, cut the nutrient and calorie values in half.

Calories

Are you overweight? Cut back a little on calories. Look here to see how a serving of the food adds to your daily total. A 5' 4", 138-lb. active woman needs about 2,200 calories each day. A 5' 10", 174-lb. active man needs about 2,900. How about you?

Total Carbohydrate

When you cut down on fat, you can eat more carbohydrates. Carbohydrates are in foods like bread, potatoes, fruits and vegetables. Choose these often! They give you more nutrients than sugars like soda pop and candy.

Dietary Fiber

Grandmother called it "roughage," but her advice to eat more is still up-to-date! That goes for both soluble and insoluble kinds of dietary fiber. Fruits, vegetables, whole-grain foods, beans and peas are all good sources and can help reduce the risk of heart disease and cancer.

Protein

Most Americans get more protein than they need. Where there is animal protein, there is also fat and cholesterol. Eat small servings of lean meat, fish and poultry. Use skim or low-fat milk, yogurt and cheese. Try vegetable proteins like beans, grains and cereals.

Vitamins & Minerals

Your goal here is 100% of each for the day. Don't count on one food to do it all. Let a combination of foods add up to a winning score.

Total Fat

Aim low: Most people need to cut back on fat! Too much fat may contribute to heart disease and cancer. Try to limit your calories from fat. For a healthy heart, choose foods with a big difference between the total number of calories and the number of calories from fat.

Saturated Fat

A new kind of fat? No — saturated fat is part of the total fat in food. It is listed separately because it's the key player in raising blood cholesterol and your risk of heart disease. Eat less!

Cholesterol

Too much cholesterol — a second cousin to fat — can lead to heart disease. Challenge yourself to eat less than 300 mg each day.

Sodium

You call it "salt," the label calls it "sodium." Either way, it may add up to high blood pressure in some people. So, keep your sodium intake low — 2,400 to 3,000 mg or less each day.*

*The AHA recommends no more than 3,000 mg sodium per day for healthy adults.

Daily Value

Feel like you're drowning in numbers? Let the Daily Value be your guide. Daily Values are listed for people who eat 2,000 or 2,500 calories each day. If you eat more, your personal daily value may be higher than what's listed on the label. If you eat less, your personal daily value may be lower.

For fat, saturated fat, cholesterol and sodium, choose foods with a low % Daily Value. For total carbohydrate, dietary fiber, vitamins and minerals, your daily value goal is to reach 100% of each.

Nutrition Facts

Serving Size ½ cup (114g)
Servings Per Container 4

Amount Per Serving

Calories 90	Calories from Fat 30

	% Daily Value*
Total Fat 3g	**5%**
Saturated Fat 0g	**0%**
Cholesterol 0mg	**0%**
Sodium 300mg	**13%**
Total Carbohydrate 13g	**4%**
Dietary Fiber 3g	**12%**
Sugars 3g	
Protein 3g	

Vitamin A	80%	•	Vitamin C	60%
Calcium	4%	•	Iron	4%

* Percent Daily Values are based on a 2,000 calorie diet. Your daily values may be higher or lower depending on your calorie needs:

	Calories	2,000	2,500
Total Fat	Less than	65g	80g
Sat Fat	Less than	20g	25g
Cholesterol	Less than	300mg	300mg
Sodium	Less than	2,400mg	2,400mg
Total Carbohydrate		300g	375g
Fiber		25g	30g

Calories per gram:
Fat 9 • Carbohydrate 4 • Protein 4

More nutrients may be listed on some labels.

g = grams (About 28 g = 1 ounce)
mg = milligrams (1,000 mg = 1 g)

Tamaño de la porción

¿Es su porción del mismo tamaño al indicado en la etiqueta? Si usted come una porción del doble del tamaño mencionado, necesita también duplicar los valores nutritivos y calóricos. Si come la mitad de la porción indicada, disminuya los valores nutritivos y calóricos a la mitad.

Calorías

¿Está usted por encima de su peso? ¡Disminuya un poco las calorías! Use como guía el número de calorías en cada porción. Seleccione alimentos bajos en calorías y en grasa.

Total de carbohidratos

Cuando usted disminuye su consumo de grasa, puede comer más carbohidratos. Los carbohidratos se encuentran en alimentos como el pan, las papas, las frutas y las verduras. ¡Selecciónelos con frecuencia! Estos le dan más nutrientes que los azúcares (sugars) como las sodas y los dulces.

Fibra dietética

El consejo de nuestras abuelas sigue siendo bueno. ¡Coma más fibra dietética! Las frutas, las verduras, los alimentos de granos integrales, los frijoles y los guisantes son todos buenas fuentes de fibra y pueden ayudarle a reducir el riesgo de enfermedades del corazón y del cáncer.

Proteínas

La mayoría de las personas consume más proteínas de las que necesita. Donde hay proteína animal, también hay grasa y colesterol. Consuma porciones pequeñas de carne magra, pescado y aves. Use leche descremada o leche, yogurt y quesos bajos en grasa. Pruebe las proteínas vegetales como los frijoles, los granos y los cereales.

Vitaminas y minerales

Su meta diaria es del 100% de cada uno. Usted puede lograrla consumiendo una amplia variedad de alimentos.

Nutrition Facts

Serving Size ½ cup (114g)
Servings Per Container 4

Amount Per Serving

Calories 90		Calories from Fat 30
		% Daily Value*
Total Fat 3g		5%
Saturated Fat 0g		0%
Cholesterol 0mg		0%
Sodium 300mg		13%
Total Carbohydrate 13g		4%
Dietary Fiber 3g		12%
Sugars 3g		
Protein 3g		

Vitamin A	80%	•	Vitamin C	60%
Calcium	4%	•	Iron	4%

* Percent Daily Values are based on a 2,000 calorie diet. Your daily values may be higher or lower depending on your calorie needs.

	Calories	2,000	2,500
Total Fat	Less than	65g	80g
Sat Fat	Less than	20g	25g
Cholesterol	Less than	300mg	300mg
Sodium	Less than	2,400mg	2,400mg
Total Carbohydrate		300g	375g
Fiber		25g	30g

Calories per gram:
Fat 9 • Carbohydrate 4 • Protein 4

Más nutrientes pueden aparecer en algunas etiquetas.

Grasa total

¡La mayoría de las personas necesita reducir el consumo de grasa! Demasiada grasa puede contribuir a las enfermedades del corazón y al cáncer. Trate de limitar las calorías de la grasa (**calories from fat**). Para un corazón sano, seleccione alimentos con una gran diferencia entre el número total de calorías y el número de calorías de la grasa.

Grasa saturada

La grasa saturada es parte de la grasa total en los alimentos. Es el ingrediente clave para elevar el nivel del colesterol en la sangre y su riesgo de enfermedades del corazón. ¡Coma menos grasa!

Colesterol

Demasiado colesterol puede ocasionar enfermedades del corazón. Comprométase a comer menos de 300 mg cada día.

Sodio

Usted la llama "sal", la etiqueta lo llama "sodio". De cualquier forma, puede contribuir a la presión arterial alta en algunas personas. Así que mantenga bajo su consumo de sodio — de 2,400 a 3,000 mg o menos cada día.*

La AHA recomienda no más de 3,000 mg de sodio por día para adultos sanos.

Valor diario (Daily Value)

Los valores diarios se indican para personas que consumen 2,000 ó 2,500 calorías diarias. Si usted necesita comer más, su valor diario puede ser más alto que los indicados en la etiqueta. Si necesita comer menos, su valor diario puede ser más bajo.

Para la grasa, la grasa saturada, el colesterol y el sodio, seleccione alimentos con un bajo % de valor diario (**% Daily Value**). Para el total de carbohidratos, la fibra dietética, las vitaminas y los minerales, su meta de valor diario es alcanzar el 100% de cada uno.

g = gramos (Para 28 g = 1 onza)
mg = miligramos (1,000 mg = 1 g)

BUYING GUIDE AND RECIPE MODIFICATIONS

With so many choices available at the grocery store, buying groceries can be confusing, but it is easy to remember that some of the best nutritional choices are found around the perimeter of the grocery store. Fresh fruits and vegetables, lowfat milk products, lean meats and lowfat cheeses can all be found on the outside aisles of the supermarket. Frozen vegetables and nonsweetened fruit juices are also good choices.

When going through aisles with candies, cookies, pastries and ice creams, just say no. Opt for simpler, lower calorie foods.

TRY	INSTEAD OF
Corn tortillas, whole wheat tortillas made with oil, pita bread, low calorie bread, bolillos	Flour tortillas, rich breads rolls
Bagels	Doughnuts
Lean beef, chicken breast, fish	Organ meats, high-fat meats such as brisket, pork
Turkey ham, lean cold cuts	Ham
Ground round or lean ground chuck, ground turkey breast	Ground beef
Egg substitute, egg whites	Eggs
Lowfat cream cheese	Cream cheese
Lowfat cheese, string cheese, Mozzarella cheese	Regular cheese

TRY	INSTEAD OF
Lowfat plain yogurt, lowfat sour cream	Sour cream
Nonfat refried beans or beans made with oil	Refried beans made with lard
Low calorie salad dressing (less than 6 gm fat per serving)	Regular mayonnaise or salad dressing
Lowfat milk	Whole milk
Tub margarine	Butter or margarine
Liquid vegetable oils	Shortening or lard
Fruits, fresh or canned in their own syrup	Fruits canned in heavy syrup
Baked tortilla chips	Regular fried tortilla chips
Cereal with less than 6 gm sucrose/serving	Sugar-rich cereals
Pretzels or air-popped corn	Chips
Animal or graham crackers, reduced-fat cookies	Cookies
Frozen yogurt or fat-free, ice cream, frozen fruit bars	Regular or Gourmet ice creams
Sugar-free gelatin	Regular desserts or gelatin
100% fruit juice	Sugared beverages

The many oils and fats available can be confusing. Although there are better fat sources than others, it is important to limit all types of fats in a healthy diet. (See also **Lowering Blood Cholesterol, Chapter One**.)

Fat Sources to Use Moderately	Fat Sources to Avoid/Use Less
Olive Oil	Lard
Canola Oil	Butter
Safflower Oil	Poultry Fat
Sunflower Oil	Beef, Pork, Veal, Lamb Fat
Soybean Oil	Coconut Oil
Corn Oil	Palm Oil
Soft tub margarines listing liquid vegetable oil as primary ingredient	Shortening, including all vegetable shortening, Solid margarine stick

At the Grocery Store

Here are some other guidelines that may help.

*   Purchase flank steak instead of skirt steak. It is leaner.

*   Brisket, choice and prime cuts of beef are all high-fat meats.

*   Avoid all organ meats. This includes liver, brains, sweetbreads, tripe and tongue.

*   The fat content of turkey is usually not labeled. Ground turkey is usually a combination of white and dark meats, skin and fat. Ask the butcher if he can grind turkey breast meat.

* All chicken parts have different fat contents. The breast is the lowest in fat, followed by the drumstick and then the thigh. Remember, always remove all skin and excess fat before cooking.

The following are better choices of meats to purchase.

Key words to remember are *round/loin* for beef, *loin/leg* for pork, lamb and veal. These words on the label indicate a lower fat content. Try to purchase *select* cuts of beef. This term will also indicate a lower fat content. Even when cooking lean meat, drain off excess juices and fat.

Beef: round tip, top round, eye of round, top loin, tenderloin and sirloin

Pork: tenderloin, boneless top loin, center loin chop

Poultry: chicken breast, skinless chicken leg, skinless turkey light meat, skinless turkey dark meat

Lamb: loin, chop, leg

Make **fish** a choice at the grocery store. Recommended fish choices include fresh or frozen fish or canned fish packed in water.

Recommended Low-Fat Food Choices at Select Fast Food Restaurants

Item	Fat (g)	Calories	Cholesterol (mg)	Sodium (mg)
Jack in the Box				
Chicken Fajita Pita				
(w/o cheese)	8	292	34	704
Taco	11	187	18	406
Taco Bell				
Bean Burrito	11	359	13	922
Bell Beefer	13	312	39	855
Taco	11	183	32	276
Soft Taco	12	228	32	516
Chicken Fajita	10	226	44	619
Pintos & Cheese				
w/ sauce	8-9	194	19	733
Steak Fajita	11	234	14	507
Tostado	11	243	18	670
Border Lights™				
Light Taco	5	140	20	NA
Light Soft Taco	5	180	25	NA
Light Taco				
Supreme™	5	160	20	NA
Light Soft Taco				
Supreme®	5	200	25	NA
Light Chicken				
Soft Taco	5	180	30	NA
Light Bean Burrito	6	330	5	NA
Light Chicken Burrito	6	290	30	NA
Light 7-layer Burrito	9	440	5	NA
Light Burrito				
Supreme®	8	350	25	NA
Light Chicken				
Burrito Supreme	10	410	65	NA
Light Taco Salad				
w/o chips	9	330	50	NA
Taco John's				
Heart Smart™				
Bean Burrito	4	294	10	642
Beef Burrito	9	309	22	591
Chicken Fajita Burrito	6	294	36	880
Chicken Fajita				
Softshell	2	149	26	639
Softshell Taco	4	165	16	406
Taco Salad	7	276	24	777

Resources for more health and nutrition information are listed on the next page with English/Spanish availability noted.

Office of Minority Health Resource Center (OMHRC)

PO Box 37337

Washington, DC 20013-7337

(800) 444-6472

Established by the federal government, the OMHRC provides a toll-free information line staffed by bilingual (English/Spanish) information specialists. Call or write for a list of publications and location of local-, state- and national-level minority health resources.

American Heart Association National Center

7272 Greenville Avenue

Dallas, TX 75231-4596

(800) USA-AHA1 or (800) 872-2421

A number of pamphlets, bulletins and booklets available for free or a small charge. Information available on general heart, high blood pressure, nutrition and exercise, risk factors, stroke, seniors and several Spanish pamphlets.

US Department of Agriculture (USDA)

Center for Nutrition Policy and Promotion

Suite 200, North Lobby 1120 20th Street NW

Washington, DC 20036

(202) 606-8000   Publications Order Line

Publications include information on the Dietary Guidelines for Americans and Food Guide Pyramid. Some bulletins are printed in Spanish.

American Dietetic Association/National Center for Nutrition and Dietetics

Consumer Nutrition Hot Line Phone (800) 366-1655

Hours from 9:00 am to 4:00 pm (Central Time) Monday-Friday

Timely recorded nutrition messages in both English and Spanish, also an opportunity to speak directly with a Registered Dietitian (English-speaking only). Several topic-specific, nutrition pamphlets available in English and Spanish.

USDA Meat and Poultry Hotline (800) 535-4555

Hours from 9:00 am to 5:00 pm (Eastern Time) Monday-Friday

Features timely recorded food safety information and the opportunity to speak directly with a home economist or dietitian.

American Seafood Institute Seafood Hotline

(800) 328-3474 from 9:00 am to 5:00 pm (Eastern Time) Monday-Friday Staff will answer questions on the purchase, preparation, storage and nutritional value of seafood products.

CHAPTER
THREE

CHAPTER THREE

THE MEXICAN KITCHEN

La Cocina Mexicana: Essential Tools and Ingredients

There are some pieces of equipment recommended for authentic Mexican cookery. Many of these kitchen utensils are available in the Hispanic sections of grocery stores or in gourmet shops. Mail order sources for recommended equipment are also included at the end of this chapter.

Griddle
Nice but not absolutely necessary for making corn or flour tortillas. An electric griddle will heat more evenly and cook more tortillas at once. If unavailable, a regular stovetop griddle will do nicely.

Lime Squeezer
Squeezes the juice out of limes and is easy to use and easy to care for. Consists of two, deep spoon-shaped pieces made of metal and joined with a hinge. One of the sides has small holes to allow juice to run out. A lime half is placed between the two pieces of metal and squeezed to release juice.

Molcajete
Lava rock used for grinding spices such as whole cumin, peppercorns and garlic. The molcajete functions as a mortar and pestle. The rough rock texture is excellent for grinding authentic spices. If unavailable, a blender may be used to grind spices. (Also see **Appetizers & Salsas**.)

Nonstick pans
Essential for any heart-healthy kitchen. Using nonstick pans helps decrease the total amount of fat used in cooking.

Rolling pin
Needed for flour tortilla preparation.

Tortilla press
Used for corn tortillas. The tortilla press consists of two hinged metal circles, preferably cast iron, 6-8 inches in diameter with a lever opposite the hinge. Corn masa dough is placed in the center of the press, and one side is lowered using the lever to form the tortilla using gentle pressure.

If unavailable, using one's hands to form the corn tortilla is also adequate.

Tortilla warmer Insulated round container with a tight fitting, insulated lid. Styrofoam tortilla warmers are very inexpensive and do a great job of keeping tortillas warm.

The following is a list of essential ingredients with which a healthy, simple Mexican meal can be prepared. These items should be well-stocked in the kitchen to help avoid last minute trips to the store.

Black pepper, whole

Cilantro

Corn tortillas

Cumin, whole

Flour

Garlic

Green Peppers

Lettuce

Lowfat Cheese

Mexican Spice Mix (whole cumin and peppercorns)

Pinto Beans

Onions

Rice

Tomatoes

Tomato Sauce

HELPFUL HINTS FOR PREPARING HEART-HEALTHY MEXICAN MEALS

Nonstick pans are essential for low-fat cooking. Food that will not stick to the pan will require far less oil or margarine. When using nonstick pans, reduce heating temperature slightly to avoid scorching foods.

Using a **molcajete** or blender, prepare a spice blend using garlic, cumin and peppercorns. Mix with a small amount of water. This will keep for about 14 days in the refrigerator. Spices will add extra flavor to low-fat foods.

"Refried" beans do not have to be fried. Prepare low-fat beans and use potato masher to achieve thick consistency. Allow excess liquid to evaporate by simmering gently. No extra fat is needed.

Corn tortillas have very little fat compared to flour tortillas. They can be prepared from a corn flour mix and are low in sodium when made without added salt. These should be used more often at the table and in recipes. One flour tortilla has more than three times as much fat as a corn tortilla.

Salsa prepared at home without added fat are a great way to enhance the flavor of many foods and add vitamins to your diet. Tomatoes and chiles are good sources of Vitamins A and C, and salsas are low in calories. Homemade salsas are lower in sodium than commercial salsas.

When **sautéing vegetables** to be used in a recipe, chop them finely and sauté using nonstick cooking spray or a very small amount of oil. Remember to reduce heating temperature and watch very closely to avoid scorching.

In preparing **"guisados,"** remove all skin and excess fat from meats. Sauté over low heat using no additional fat, and drain excess fat before adding other ingredients.

Use **baked tortillas** for making tostadas, chips, chalupas and tacos. They taste great!

Experiment with different **lowfat cheese** for Mexican dishes. Or, mix a lowfat cheese with a small quantity of regular cheese, lowering the overall fat content.

Eliminate use of lard and shortening. Oils and soft tub margarines can be substituted for these in most recipes. Liquid margarines are good choices when used in small quantities.

Adding **fresh vegetables** to beans, rice and vermicelli will add more vitamins.

Prepare **rice and pasta dishes** with only a small amount of oil. Mexican rice can also be prepared by steaming rice instead of frying and adding all the usual spices for a great taste.

Flour tortillas can be made with oil instead of shortening. **Whole wheat** tortillas made with oil are even better because they contain fiber and other healthy nutrients.

Do not add extra ingredients such as mayonnaise and sour cream to avocadoes when making guacamole. These condiments add many more calories to a high-calorie food. Add fresh vegetables such as onions and tomatoes, or salsa and lime juice. Guacamole should only be consumed occasionally. It is a very high-fat food.

When cooking **pinto beans**, add only small amounts of fat. It is unnecessary to add large pieces of salt pork or many slices of bacon to beans while cooking. Adding one slice of bacon and a small amount of oil will give flavor, but not excess fat. Try adding olive oil and a variety of other vegetables such as celery, carrots, onions, cilantro and tomatoes. They add powerful **nutrients and flavor** to pinto beans.

For a diet with restricted **salt** intake, omit salt and change salty ingredients in recipes. Note the sodium content of each recipe before preparing. Most are low to moderate in sodium, but there are a few that are high in sodium. A dietitian can suggest other options as well.

GLOSSARY

Achiote   *a-chee-OE-te*
Spice used by Caribbean Hispanics. Similar to saffron in color.

Adobado   *a-doe-BA-doe*
Sauce made with chiles, onions, and other spices used in braising meats.

Albondiga   *al-BON-dee-ga*
Small meatballs, often used in soups. Can also be a fish patty.

Arroz   *a-ROES*
Rice.

Bolillo   *boe-LEE-oe*
Small Mexican hard roll, similar to French bread.

Burrito   *boo-REE-toe*
Meat or beans wrapped in tortilla, usually flour. May include cheese. Sometimes fried.

Calabaza   *ka-la-BA-sa*
Universal name for many types of squash.

Caliente   *kal-ee-EN-te*
Hot.

Caldo   *KAL-doe*
Soup or broth.

Camarón   *ka-ma-RON*
Shrimp.

Carne   *CAR-ne*
Refers to edible meat such as beef, pork or chicken.

Chalupa   *cha-LEW-pa*
Crisp tortilla layered with beans, cheese, lettuce and tomatoes.

Chipotle   *chee-POE-tle*
Smoked jalapeno in tomato sauce.

Cilantro   *see-LAN-troe*
Chinese parsley or coriander. Herb used in many Mexican dishes. Choose it bright green with firm, fresh leaves. Store in refrigerator with stems in water.

Carne Guisada   *CAR-ne gee-SA-da*
Braised meat prepared in a spicy tomato gravy sauce.

Chiles   *CHEE-les*
Hot peppers, ranging in flavor from mild to very hot. May be purchased fresh, canned or dried. Includes jalapeno, serrano, anaheim.

Chorizo   *choe-REE-soe*
Sausage made with spices and vinegar.

Comino   *koe-MEE-noe*
Spice used in many Mexican dishes. Cumin; may be whole or ground.

Dorado   *doe-RA-doe*
Browned to a golden color.

Elote   *e-LOE-te*
Corn.

Enchiladas   *en-chee-LA-das*
Meat, cheese or vegetables rolled in a corn tortilla and baked in a sauce, usually chile or tomatillo.

Encilantrado   *en-see-LAN-tra-doe*
Dish prepared with a cilantro sauce.

Empanadas   *em-pa-NA-das*
Turnovers, usually dessert type. Can also be meat.

Escabeche   *es-ca-BE-che*
Spicy pickling solution for jalapeños and other vegetables used for preserving and adding flavor. Contains garlic and vinegar among other ingredients.

Epazote   *e-pa-SOE-te*
Spice used in cooking Mexican rice or beans. Choose firm, brownish leaves, and store in refrigerator in water.

Fajitas   *fa-HEE-tas*
Beef skirt steak.

Fideo   *fee-DAE-oe*
Vermicelli.

Flan   *FLAN*
Spanish style custard with caramelized topping.

Fresca   *FRES-ka*
Fresh.

Garbanzo   *gar-BAN-zoe*
Chickpeas.

Gazpacho   *gaz-PA-choe*
Tomato-based cold Spanish soup.

Guizado   *gee-SA-doe*
Method of preparation for meats. Meats are sautéed and prepared in a spicy tomato-based gravy.

Hongos   *ON-goes*
Mushrooms

Jalapeño   *ha-la-PEN-yoe*
Medium hot chile pepper. Can be purchased canned or fresh.

Jicama   *HEE-ka-ma*
Root-type vegetable usually eaten raw. Like a radish but sweeter, its outer grey-brown skin is removed before eating. Choose it firm with no dark spots. Store in refrigerator.

Mango   *MAN-goe*
Tropical fruit, rich in Vitamin A and C. Oval shaped, greenish-yellow fruit. Ripe fruit has no brown spots and yields to gentle pressure.

Manzana   *man-SAN-a*
Apple.

Marisco   *ma-REES-coe*
Seafood.

Masa   *MA-sa*
Dough, may be corn or flour.

Masa Harina   *MA-sa a-REE-na*
Corn flour, used for making tamales and corn tortillas.

Mexican Spice Mix
Blend of whole cumin and peppercorns.

Molcajete   *mol-ca-HE-te*
Lava rock "mortar and pestle" used since ancient times to grind spices.

Nopalito   *no-pa-LEE-toe*
Young cactus leaves. Eaten raw or cooked.

Pan   *PAN*
Bread.

Papitas   *pa-PEE-tas*
Potatoes.

Pescado   *pes-KA-doe*
Fish.

Piña   *PEEN-ya*
Pineapple.

Platano   *PLA-ta-noe*
Banana.

Pollo   *POE-yoe*
Chicken.

Posole   *poe-SOE-le*
Chile stew made with meats, hominy and chile.

Quesadilla   *KAE-sa-dee-ya*
Tortillas prepared with cheese.

Repollo *re-POE-yoe*
Cabbage.

Salsa *SAL-sa*
Garnish or sauce made in different ways, usually tomato-based. May be cooked or fresh.

Semita *se-MEE-ta*
Sweetened bread made with anise.

Sopa *SOE-pa*
Soup or pasta dish.

Suiza *SUE-ee-sa*
Dish prepared with a green tomatillo sauce and sometimes sour cream.

Taco *TA-koe*
Crisp tortilla filled with spicy meat, garnished with lettuce, tomatoes and cheese.

Tamales *ta-MA-les*
Corn flour masa cooked with spicy meat filling in corn shucks.

Tomatillos *toe-ma-TEE-yoes*
Small green tomato-like vegetables with a tart citrus-like flavor. To choose, lift outer covering and look for bright, green-yellow color with brown spots.

Tortas *TOR-tas*
Beans and cheese warmed on French bread-type rolls.

Tortillas *tore-TEE-yas*
Thin, round bread cooked on griddle. May be corn or flour.

Verde *VER-de*
Green.

Verduras *ver-DOO-ras*
Vegetables.

CHILES

The use of chiles in traditional Hispanic dishes can be dated back to the Ancient Mayan and Aztec Indians. In his journal, Columbus made note of the use of chiles by the natives, recording remarks about the tastiness of this food new to Europeans (Toussaint-Samat 515).

The tradition of using varied chiles in Mexican and Mexican-American cooking continues and therefore requires some advice. While not all chiles are hot enough to cause problems, it is safer to handle all chiles with caution. Use gloves when slicing chiles, especially fresh ones. Some canned chiles can be as hot or hotter than fresh chiles. The most potent part of chiles is the seeds and the inner membranes. These should be removed before preparing a dish with fresh or canned chiles unless otherwise specified. Should you decide not to use gloves, avoid rubbing your eyes with your hands as the potent oils in the chiles will burn. The best rule is to use caution, and if in doubt, use gloves to handle all but the mildest chiles.

Anaheim
About 4-5 inches long, 1 1/2 inches wide, medium green in color, has a "twisted" appearance. The most common chile available. Available fresh and canned. Also called green chiles in many recipes. Very mild in taste.

Chipotle
Jalapeño peppers that have been smoked and canned in a red chile sauce. Usually chopped.

Jalapeño
2-3 inches long, 1 inch wide, deep green in color. Very hot. Available fresh, canned and "en escabeche."

Poblano
4-5 inches long, deep green in color and hot. Used for chiles rellenos and in salsas.

Serrano
1-2 inches long, 1/2 inch wide, deep green in color. Very hot. Most commonly found fresh. Used often in PICO DE GALLO.

Many recipes call for charred chiles, which give a delicious, smoked flavor to authentic Mexican dishes. While there exist many ways to char chiles, the following guidelines may be helpful.

Prepare chiles by rinsing in warm water. Place on cookie sheet. Preheat broiler unit. Place chiles under broiler for 6-8 minutes or until blistered. Turn frequently until all are blistered evenly. Remove from broiler, place between clean, damp towels, or in a paper bag for 10 minutes. Remove from bag and peel carefully. Peel should come off easily. Remove stem, veins and seeds.

Another method involves charring the chiles on a hot griddle or frying pan. Place the cleaned chiles in the hot griddle or frying pan and turn to char all surfaces evenly. Using a pancake turner helps exert pressure on the chile for even charring. Place between clean, damp towels or in a paper bag for 10 minutes. Remove and peel carefully.

The method that probably results in the most flavorful chile involves using the grill, preferably with a fragrant wood burning such as mesquite. Place chiles in hot area of grill, turning carefully to char all surfaces evenly. Remove and place between clean damp towels or in a paper bag for 10 minutes. Peel carefully.

Work Cited

Toussant-Samat, Maguelone. HISTORY OF FOOD. Cambridge: Blackwell Publishers, 1993.

SPECIALTY SUPPLIERS

Brown's Edgewood Gardens Herb Catalog
2611 Corrine Drive
Orlando, FL 32803
(407) 896-3203
Fresh cilantro plants, fresh Mexican oregano, fresh garlic plants.
Minimum Order $10.00. Catalog is $3.00.

Fiesta Mart
#19 1005 Blalock
Houston, TX 77055
(713) 461-9664
Attn: Tom Stamas, International Foods Store.
They do not do mail order but are great to visit if you're in the
area.   They offer cooking classes.

Mellinger's
2310 West South Range Road
North Lima, OH 44452-9731
Mail order source for tomatillo seeds.

Mexican Products and Spices Company
RR1 Box 1191
La Feria, TX 78559
(210) 636-1288
Individual and wholesale orders. They have a flyer and product
list. Specialties include many Mexican spices.

New Mexico Catalog
1700 Shalem Colony Trail
PO Box 261
Fairacres, NM 88033-0261
(800) 678-0585
Mail order source for posole and molcajete.

New Mexico Connection de Nuevo Mexico
2833 Rhode Island NE
Albuquerque, NM 87110
(505) 292-5493 or (800) 933-2736
Free catalog. Great source for masa harina, corn shucks, some spices, fresh chiles, and dried posole.

The Quaker Oats Company
P.O. Box 9003
Chicago, IL 60604-9003
Manufacturer of masa harina corn tortilla mix. Available at many grocery stores.

Rafal Spice Company
2521 Russell
Detroit, MI 48207
(313) 259-6373
Chile peppers, chili powders, Mexican oregano, salsa, and hot sauce extracts, as well as pepper grinders and garlic presses. Free catalog.

Texas Edibles & Special Gifts
4004 W. Jasmine St.
P.O. Box 2062
Pearland, TX 77588-2062
(800) 252-6838
Mail order salsas made from fresh ingredients with no artificial ingredients or preservatives. Distributes a green tomato sauce that is an excellent substitute for the tomatillo sauce used in many recipes.

MENU IDEAS

Try some of these menu suggestions the next time you're having a party. Most of the recipes are found in this book, HEALTHY MEXICAN COOKING. Only recipes which do not appear in this book are marked with an asterisk.

CHRISTMAS EVE FIESTA

Mexican Health Dip
Tamales
Tia's Beans
Carrot and Cilantro Salad
Empanadas
Virgin Margaritas*

CINCO DE MAYO

Burritos Verde
Lime Rice
South Texas Squash
Kahlua Parfait

NEW YEAR'S DAY

Texas Caviar
Baked Tortilla Chips
Chicken Tamales
Tia's Beans
Southwestern Rice Casserole
Coyotitas

TEX-MEX SPECIAL

Cabbage Salad
Carne Guidsada
Tia's Beans
The Best Mexican Rice
Fresh Corn Tortillas
Mango Flan

COMPANY'S COMING

Jicama Salad
King Ranch Casserole
Mexican Fiesta Salad
Bolillos
Strawberry Banana Parfait

BRUNCH

Pinto Bean Salad
Onion and Tomato Relish
Tortas
The Best Mexican Rice
Marinated Fruit Dessert

HALLOWEEN FRIGHT NIGH

Baked Tortilla Chips
Fiesta del Sol Dip
Carrot Sticks*
White Chili
Fresh Corn Tortillas
Apples*

APPETIZERS
&
SALSAS

APPETIZERS AND SALSAS

A NOTE ABOUT ROASTING VEGETABLES

The process of roasting vegetables is becoming more common in American cooking, and has been used in authentic Mexican cooking for many years.

When you roast a vegetable, the natural vegetable sugar caramelizes, enhancing the flavor of the vegetable. Roasting can be done over an open flame such as a mesquite grill or can be done in a very hot oven or even in a very hot skillet. Each process determines the final flavor of the vegetable, and while it must be done with care, roasting vegetables is easy to do and adds a unique flavor to authentic Mexican dishes.

If roasting in the oven, line the pan you will be using with aluminum foil for easier cleanup. Watch the roasting vegetables closely because the oven temperature is very, very hot. Using metal tongs, carefully turn vegetable to assure even roasting. Use caution when removing from the oven, as the pan will be extremely hot.

The results will be delicious!

THE MOLCAJETE

Use of the molcajete, a grinding tool, dates back to the ancient civilizations of the Indians. An authentic molcajete is made of lava rock, the coarse texture being important to its grinding function.

Two pieces of this lava rock are used. The bottom part is a bowl-shaped rock used together with a cone-shaped rock to strike the spices being ground. The molcajete is most likely the ancient predecessor of today's mortar and pestle.

The most common spices ground in the molcajete are whole cumin seeds, whole pepper and garlic cloves. The blend of these special spices is what gives Mexican food its wonderful characteristic flavor and unequaled aroma. Occasionally, the molcajete is used both to prepare and serve guacamole and salsas. The larger ones are often used for different purposes, since they come in different sizes and vary slightly in shape.

A somewhat similar kitchen tool called the *metate* is used to "stone grind" corn for making tortillas, tamales and other ground corn foods. It was also used by ancient Indian cultures. The metate is also made from lava rock but has a rectangular, sloped shape, much larger that the molcajete, to allow for the hard, downward strokes used to grind corn.

Molcajetes are wonderful pieces of kitchen equipment every Mexican cook requires. Included earlier in **Chapter 3** is a source guide for purchasing a molcajete, but if you cannot find one, there is also a recipe using a blender to prepare these spices. It will yield a similar great taste.

BEAN DIP

Dip de Frijol

3   cups TIA'S BEANS (page 202)
1/2   cup jalapeño slices, seeded

Using a potato masher or food processor, process slightly drained beans to smooth consistency. Carefully chop jalapeño slices into small pieces, then blend with beans. Serve cold or warm in microwave for a hot dip.

<u>Serves 6</u>

Nutrient Analysis: 1 serving
62 Calories, 3 g Fat, 6 g Fiber, 230 mg Sodium, 1 g Sat Fat, 2 mg Cholesterol
Diabetic Exchange: 1 1/2 BREAD

CHILE CHEESE TORTILLAS

Chile Quesadillas

3	ounces lowfat Monterey Jack cheese, grated
3	ounces regular Monterey Jack cheese, grated
1/2	cup California green chiles, diced, well drained
6	corn tortillas

Mix cheeses together.

Warm tortillas on heated griddle. Sprinkle grated cheeses and chilies on each open-faced tortilla. Warm on griddle until cheese melts. Fold in half. Serve with homemade salsa.

Serves 3

Nutrient Analysis: 1 serving
315 Calories, 15 g Fat , 2 g Fiber, 334 mg Sodium, 3.5 g Sat Fat, 39 mg Cholesterol
Diabetic Exchange: 2 BREAD, 2 MEAT, 2 FAT

CREAMY SALSA DIP

Dip de Salsa con Queso

1 cup 1% lowfat cottage cheese
2 tablespoons light cream cheese
1/2 cup salsa

Place all ingredients in a blender or food processor. Cover and process until smooth and creamy. Refrigerate for at least 4 hours to allow flavors to blend.

<u>Serves 4</u>

Nutrient Analysis: 1 serving
20 Calories, 0 g Fat, 1 g Fiber ,130 mg Sodium, tr Sat Fat, 0 mg Cholesterol
Diabetic Exchange: 1 MEAT

FIESTA DEL SOL DIP

Dip de Fiesta del Sol

1	pint lowfat small curd cottage cheese
1/2	cup green chiles, diced
2	tomatoes, seeded and diced
1/2	cup green onions, diced
1/2	teaspoon salt
1/2	teaspoon Worcestershire sauce
3	dashes hot sauce

Blend all ingredients together in a blender or food processor until smooth. Refrigerate about 4 hours or overnight to allow flavors to blend.

Serves 8

Nutrient Analysis: 1 serving
65 Calories, 1 g Fat, 1 g Fiber, 630 mg Sodium, 1 g Sat Fat, 3 mg Cholesterol
Diabetic Exchange: 1/2 VEGETABLE, 1 MEAT

GRILLED QUESADILLA

Quesadilla Parrillada

These appetizers can be used for barbeques. They are low in fat and delicious!

4	**corn tortillas**
4	**ounces part skim Mozzarella cheese, shredded**
1/2	**cup green onions, chopped finely**
3	**tablespoons freshly squeezed lime juice, strained**

Place tortillas on heated grill to warm slightly. Warm on both sides. On each open-faced tortilla, place 1/4 cheese and 1/4 onions. Sprinkle lime juice on each tortilla. Warm on grill until cheese has melted. Fold in half to serve as appetizer.

<u>4 servings</u>

Nutrient Analysis: 1 serving
140 Calories, 5 g Fat, 1 g Fiber, 135 mg Sodium, 3 g Sat Fat, 16 mg Cholesterol
Diabetic Exchange: 1 BREAD, 1 MEAT, 1 FAT

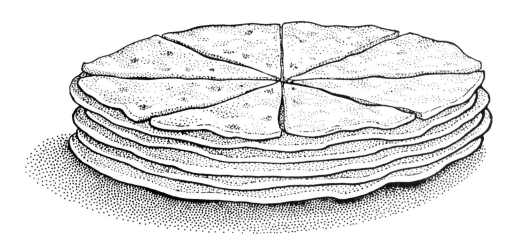

HOMEMADE BEAN DIP

Dip de Frijol Casero

2	cups cooked pinto beans, drained
1/2	cup canned green chiles, diced
1/2	cup tomato sauce, no salt added
1/3	cup onion, chopped
1	tablespoon apple cider vinegar
5	drops hot sauce

Combine all ingredients in a food processor or blender, and process until smooth. Refrigerate 4-5 hours or overnight, allowing flavors to blend. Serve warm or cold with baked tortilla chips or pita crisps.

<u>12 servings</u>

Nutrient Analysis: 1 serving
55 Calories, 1 g Fat, 2 g Fiber, 175 mg Sodium, tr g Sat Fat, 1 mg Cholesterol
Diabetic Exchange: 1/2 VEGETABLE, 1/2 BREAD

MUSHROOMS

Hongos

6   **large mushrooms**
1/4 **cup onions, finely chopped**
2   **teaspoons reduced calorie tub margarine, divided**
2   **tablespoons diced California green chiles**
2   **tablespoons fat-free cream cheese**
1/4 **teaspoon salt**
1/8 **teaspoon black pepper**

Wash mushrooms and separate stems from caps. Chop stems finely. In a small nonstick skillet, add 1 teaspoon margarine and sauté mushroom stems along with onions. Add chiles, warm for 1-2 minutes.

Remove from heat and mix with cream cheese. Blend in salt and pepper. Set aside.

In a separate microwave bowl, combine mushroom caps along with remaining margarine. Microwave on high for approximately 30 seconds and stir. Continue this process two more times. Remove from microwave and allow to cool.

Stuff mushroom caps with cream cheese mixture and heat in a 350° oven for approximately 5-10 minutes to warm through.

3 servings

Nutrient Analysis: 1 serving
20 Calories, 1 g Fat, 1 g Fiber, 240 mg Sodium, 0 g Sat Fat, 0 mg Cholesterol
Diabetic Exchange: 1/2 VEGETABLE

JALAPEÑO MUSHROOMS

Hongos con Jalapeños

4   cups jalapeños en escabeche (see GLOSSARY for description), liquid included
4   cups small whole mushrooms, cleaned

Add mushrooms to jalapeños with juice in a bowl with tight fitting lid. Marinate overnight, or longer, if desired. The longer they marinate, the hotter they get!

Serve cold or room temperature.

<u>8 servings</u>

Nutrient Analysis: 1 serving
25 Calories, 1 g Fat, 2 g Fiber, 450 mg Sodium, 0 g Sat Fat, 0 mg Cholesterol
Diabetic Exchange: 1 VEGETABLE

MEXICAN HEALTH DIP

Dip Mejicano Saludable

The purple cabbage makes a nice centerpiece surrounded by fresh vegetables used for dipping.

2	**cups plain nonfat yogurt**
1/4	**cup prepared salsa or MORNING SAUCE (page 71)**
1/2	**cup green onions, chopped**
1	**head purple cabbage**

Mix together yogurt, salsa and onions. Blend well and refrigerate overnight.

Just before serving, rinse cabbage and remove center, leaving about 1" around edges. Pour dip into cavity and serve with lots of fresh vegetables.

<u>Serves 8</u>

Nutrient Analysis: 1 serving
20 Calories, 0 g Fat, 0 g Fiber, 98 mg Sodium, tr Sat Fat, 1 mg Cholesterol
Diabetic Exchange: 1/2 MILK

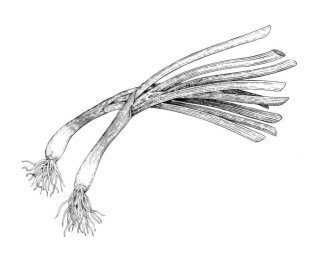

DELICIOUS NACHOS

Nachos Deliciosos

6   corn tortillas
4   ounces lowfat Mozzarella cheese, grated
1/2   cup California green chiles, diced and drained
Nonstick cooking spray

Preheat oven to 500°.

Immerse tortillas in water and let drain briefly. Stack the tortillas and cut them into 6 wedges for nachos. Spray baking sheets with nonstick cooking spray. Place wedges in a single layer on baking sheet.

Bake in 500° oven for about 8 minutes, turning once after about 4 minutes. Watch carefully—when baking at this temperature foods tend to burn rapidly. Reduce oven temperature to 350°.

Top with grated cheese and return to 350° oven briefly until cheese melts. Just before serving, top with diced green chiles.

<u>Serves 6</u>

Nutrient Analysis: 1 serving
110 Calories, 3 g Fat, 1 g Fiber, 152 mg Sodium, tr g Sat Fat , 7 mg Cholesterol
Diabetic Exchange: 1 BREAD, 1/2 MEAT, 1/2 FAT

PICANTE DIP

Dip de Picante

This recipe demonstrates that you don't have to cut out all fat in the diet; small changes made for a lifetime will make a difference.

8   ounces lowfat cream cheese
4   ounces picante sauce or homemade salsa

In a medium bowl, mix softened cream cheese with picante sauce. Stir until well blended. Serve with baked tostadas, garlic pita or fresh vegetables.

<u>8 servings</u>

Nutrient Analysis: 1 serving
40 Calories, 2 g Fat, 0 g Fiber, 193 mg Sodium, 0 g Sat Fat, 0 mg Cholesterol
Diabetic Exchange: 1/2 FAT

STUFFED JALAPEÑOS

Jalapeños Relleños

12	**jalapeños en escabeche***
3	**ounces lowfat cream cheese**
1/2	**cup finely shredded lowfat sharp Cheddar cheese**
1/4	**cup green onions, finely chopped**

Carefully cut each jalapeño in half. Under running water, rinse out seeds and remove stems and veins. Set on tray.

In a small mixing bowl, mix cheeses and onions.

Use a small spoon to stuff each jalapeño half with cheese mixture. Serve cold, or warm in a 350° oven until cheeses have slightly melted.

Serves 12

Nutrient Analysis: 1 serving
55 Calories, 2 g Fat, 1 g Fiber, 63 mg Sodium, 1 g Sat Fat, 5 mg Cholesterol
Diabetic Exchange: 1/4 VEGETABLE, 1/2 FAT

* Whole, canned jalapeños will also work.

TEXAS CAVIAR

In the South, it is said to be good luck for the coming year to eat blackeyed peas on New Year's Day. Serve this dish with baked tortilla chips for a great appetizer.

2   16-ounce can blackeyed peas, rinsed and drained
1   cup onions, chopped
1/2   cup cilantro, chopped
1 1/2 cups picante sauce or homemade salsa

Combine ingredients. Chill to allow flavors to blend.

Serves 8

Nutrient Analysis: 1 serving
120 Calories, 1 g Fat, 3 g Fiber, 659 mg Sodium, tr g Sat Fat, 0 mg Cholesterol
Diabetic Exchange: 1 BREAD, 1/2 VEGETABLE

BLENDER MEXICAN SPICE MIX

Especias Mejicanas en la Licuadora

In the traditional Mexican kitchen, the molcajete, a volcanic rock grinding tool, is used to grind cumin, pepper and garlic. This spice mix will keep in the refrigerator for about 2 weeks!

4   **tablespoons Mexican Spice Mix***
4   **cloves garlic**
1   **cup water**
or
3   **tablespoons cumin**
1 1/2 **teaspoons whole black pepper (or to taste)**
4   **cloves garlic**
1   **cup water**

Add all ingredients to blender container. Blend spices until finely ground.

Nutrient Analysis: 1 recipe
90 Calories, 4 g Fat, 2 g Fiber, 33 mg Sodium, tr Sat Fat, 0 mg Cholesterol
Diabetic Exchange: None

* Available in the Hispanic section of grocery stores or through mail order sources...see pages 44-45.

CHIPOTLE SAUCE

Salsa Chipotle

Chipotle peppers are actually smoked jalapeños in a red chile sauce. They make a wonderful hot salsa.

1   8-ounce can tomato sauce, no added salt
4   chipotle peppers, with sauce (from can)

Add ingredients to blender container or food processor. Puree until smooth.

<u>8 servings</u>

Nutrient Analysis: 1 serving
12 Calories, 0 g Fat, 0 g Fiber, 57 mg Sodium, 0 g Sat Fat, 0 mg Cholesterol
Diabetic Exchange: 1/2 VEGETABLE

DENVER CORN RELISH

Condimento de Maiz Denver

This is my version of the corn relish a restaurant in Denver served with our meal.

4	tablespoons sugar
1	teaspoon ground turmeric
3/4	teaspoon ground celery seeds
1/4	cup white vinegar
1/4	cup water
1	tablespoon cornstarch
1/4	cup purple onion, chopped finely
1	10-ounce package frozen corn, no salt added
2	tablespoons green pepper, chopped
2	tablespoons cilantro, chopped finely
1	small tomato, seeded and diced

In a microwave safe dish, combine sugar, turmeric, celery seed and vinegar. Microwave on high for about 1 1/2 minutes. Combine water and cornstarch in a cup with a spout and mix thoroughly. Using a wire whisk, add cornstarch to warmed vinegar mixture. Return to microwave for about 1 minute, or until mixture begins to bubble and thicken.

Add onion, corn, green pepper, cilantro and tomatoes. Mix well. Refrigerate. Serve cold as garnish with meals.

<u>Serves 6</u>

Nutrient Analysis: 1 serving
83 Calories, 0 g Fat, 1 g Fiber, 4 mg Sodium, 0 g Sat Fat, 0 mg Cholesterol
Diabetic Exchange: 1 BREAD (does contain sugar)

POBLANO CORN RELISH

Maiz con Chile Poblano

Excellent and nonfat!

2	**fresh Poblano chiles**
1	**small onion, diced**
1	**clove garlic, finely chopped**
2	**cups frozen corn kernels**
2	**tablespoons cilantro, chopped**
1/4	**teaspoon salt**
1/4	**teaspoon pepper**

Nonstick cooking spray

Preheat oven to 500°. Rinse Poblano chiles and prepare baking sheet with aluminum foil. Place on baking sheet and roast, occasionally turning until skin has completely blistered. Immediately place chiles between damp, clean kitchen towel and set aside.

In a skillet sprayed with nonstick cooking spray, sauté onions and garlic until onions are translucent. Add frozen corn kernels and continue to warm about 10 minutes.

Meanwhile, remove chiles from towel and peel off outer skin. Remove stem and seeds. Chop chile into small pieces. Add chile, cilantro, salt and pepper to corn mixture and heat for about five minutes more. Serve warm or cold.

Serves 8

Nutrient Analysis: 1 serving
45 Calories, tr Fat, 1 g Fiber, 69 mg Sodium, tr Sat Fat, 0 mg Cholesterol
Diabetic Exchange: 1/2 VEGETABLE

EASY SMOKED SALSA

Salsa Ahumada Facil

This salsa has a unique smoked flavor. Try it with baked chips or pita.

1	**pound ripe red tomatoes**
4	**fresh California chiles**
1	**teaspoon salt (or to taste)**

Wash tomatoes thoroughly.

On a very hot griddle, cook tomatoes until the skin becomes slightly charred, turning frequently to allow skin to char evenly. As soon as tomatoes are evenly charred, immerse in ice water, taking care not to allow skin to burst.

Lower heat on griddle slightly, and proceed to heat the chiles until evenly charred. Using tongs, place chiles in a slightly damp, clean dishcloth. This will help loosen the skin for peeling.

Peel the tomatoes, and place them in a bowl. Carefully peel chiles, remove seeds and veins, and discard charred peels. Mix together and crush until a thick consistency is achieved. Add salt and blend well.

Serve with baked tortilla chips.

<u>Serves 4</u>

Nutrient Analysis: 1 serving
40 Calories, 0 g Fat, 2 g Fiber, 130 mg Sodium, 0 g Sat Fat, 0 mg Cholesterol
Diabetic Exchange: 1 VEGETABLE

FAT-FREE RED CHILI SAUCE

Salsa de Chile Colorado Sin Grasa

This is Aunt Edna's special recipe and a great nonfat sauce that can be used for enchiladas or to mix with vegetables.

1/4	**cup flour**
2	**teaspoons red chili powder (or to taste)**
2	**cups water**
1/2	**teaspoon garlic powder**
1/2	**teaspoon ground cumin**
1/2	**teaspoon onion powder**
1/2	**teaspoon black pepper**
1/2	**teaspoon salt**

Dash paprika

Add flour to a large nonstick skillet. Over medium heat, slowly brown flour, stirring often. Flour must be carefully watched to prevent scorching. The flour will turn a sandy brown color when it is done.

Remove from heat. Add chili powder and blend well.

Return to heat and gradually add water, beating with wire whisk to prevent lumps. After all water has been added, add remaining spices and salt. Bring to a boil, reduce heat and simmer for 10-15 minutes to allow flavors to blend.

Serves 8

Nutrient Analysis: 1 serving
18 Calories, tr Fat , tr Fiber, 140 mg Sodium, 0 g Sat Fat, 0 mg Cholesterol
Diabetic Exchange: FREE

JALAPEÑO SAUCE

Salsa Jalapeño

1	small onion, chopped
1	clove garlic, minced
2	cups canned tomatoes, undrained, no salt added
1/4	teaspoon oregano
1/4	teaspoon salt
1/2	cup canned jalapeño slices, chopped

Nonstick cooking spray

Prepare a large nonstick skillet with nonstick cooking spray. Using low heat, sauté onions and garlic until onions are clear. Add tomatoes and "crush" using a fork or potato masher until tomatoes are in small pieces. Add spices and jalapeños. Bring to a boil. Lower heat and simmer for 15-20 minutes, stirring frequently. This sauce can be served warm or cold — but it is caliente (hot)!!

Serves 8

Nutrient Analysis: 1 serving
35 Calories, 1 g Fat, 1 g Fiber, 74 mg Sodium, tr Sat Fat, 0 mg Cholesterol
Diabetic Exchange: 1 VEGETABLE

MORNING SAUCE

Salsa Manana

This is my mother-in-law's signature sauce. Tasty when used on meats, eggs, vegetables and tamales, it improves with age and freezes well. Many of the recipes in this book have been prepared using this very versatile, mild salsa.

1	**green pepper, seeded and finely chopped**
1	**onion, finely chopped**

Nonstick cooking spray

2	**14-ounce cans stewed tomatoes, crushed, undrained**
2	**14-ounce cans stewed tomatoes, no salt added, crushed, undrained**
3	**cloves garlic**
1	**teaspoon fresh cumin**
1	**cup cilantro, chopped finely, stems removed**
1	**teaspoon salt**
1	**teaspoon black pepper**

In a nonstick Dutch oven coated with nonstick cooking spray, saute chopped pepper and onions until onions are translucent. Add tomatoes, including liquid, and stir to blend well.

Using molcajete, grind cumin and garlic, adding a small amount of water to loosen spices and pour into sauce. Add remaining seasonings and cilantro and bring to a boil. Reduce heat and simmer on low for about 1 to 1 1/2 hours to allow flavors to blend.

<u>32 servings</u>

Nutrient Analysis: 1 serving
20 Calories, 0 g Fat, 1 g Fiber, 131 mg Sodium, tr Sat Fat, 0 mg Cholesterol
Diabetic Exchange: 1/2 VEGETABLE

PICO DE GALLO

A very common relish in Texas, we use it as an accompaniment for beef, chicken and even seafood. Pico de Gallo is low in sodium and adds lots of flavor to foods.

3	**medium tomatoes, seeded and chopped**
2/3	**cup cilantro, chopped**
1/2	**small onion, chopped**

Juice of 1-2 medium limes
Fresh jalapeno or serrano chile, chopped (optional)

Mix all ingredients. Use as relish or side dish. Keeps about 2 days refrigerated but is best if used fresh.

<u>6 servings</u>

Nutrient Analysis: 1 serving
20 Calories, 0 g Fat, 1 g Fiber, 7 mg Sodium, 0 g Sat Fat, 0 mg Cholesterol
Diabetic Exchange: 1 VEGETABLE

RED CHILI SAUCE

Salsa de Chile Colorado

This recipe is for a basic chili sauce to be used for enchiladas or other vegetable dishes.

2	tablespoons oil
2	tablespoons all-purpose flour
1 1/2	teaspoons red chili powder
1	cup water
1/2	teaspoon salt
1	garlic clove
1/2	teaspoon cumin seed or to taste

Mix flour and oil in a large nonstick skillet, making a paste. Allow to brown slowly over medium heat. Stir frequently. Flour will turn a sandy brown color. Do not allow to smoke. Add chile powder and remove from heat. Slowly add water, beating with wire whisk to make a smooth gravy. Return to heat. In molcajete, grind garlic and cumin. Add water to loosen spices. Add spices and salt to gravy. Simmer for at least 15 minutes to allow flavors to blend.

<u>Serves 4</u>

Nutrient Analysis: 1 serving
81 Calories, 7 g Fat, tr Fiber, 143 mg Sodium, 1 g Sat Fat, 0 mg Cholesterol
Diabetic Exchange: 1 BREAD, 2 FAT

SALSA FRESCA

This sauce is easy because you simply put all the ingredients into a blender. It can be frozen or kept 4-5 days in the refrigerator.

3	**cloves garlic, minced**
1/2	**cup onion, chopped**
1	**jalapeño, seeded**
1/2	**cup cilantro, stems removed**
4	**tomatoes, cut into quarters**
2	**tablespoons fresh lime juice**

Combine all ingredients in blender or food processor until desired consistency is achieved.

<u>8 servings</u>

Nutrient Analysis: 1 serving
24 Calories, 0 g Fat, 1 g Fiber, 6 mg Sodium, 0 g Sat Fat, 0 mg Cholesterol
Diabetic Exchange: 1 VEGETABLE

BURNT SALSA

Salsa Quemada

Roasting the tomatoes and chiles over a mesquite fire makes the flavor even better!

4	**tomatoes**
2	**Serrano chiles**
1	**clove garlic**
1/2	**teaspoon salt**
1/2	**cup water**

Cut tomatoes in half and remove seeds. Cut Serrano chiles and remove seeds and stems. Add tomatoes and chiles to skillet and "roast" over medium heat until well cooked, but not burned. This should take about 30 minutes.

Add tomatoes, chiles, garlic and salt to a blender or food processor and blend to desired consistency. Add water and process again.

Cool slightly and refrigerate 3-4 hours to allow flavors to blend.

<u>Serves 8</u>

Nutrient Analysis: 1 serving
16 Calories, tr Fat, 1 g Fiber, 112 mg Sodium, tr Sat Fat, 0 mg Cholesterol
Diabetic Exchange: FREE

GREEN SAUCE

Salsa Verde

10	ounces tomatillos (a medium tomatillo is about one ounce)
1	fresh Anaheim chile
1/4	cup chopped onion
3	corn tortillas, torn in small pieces
3	cloves garlic
4	ounces fresh spinach (about 3 cups, chopped)
3	cups low-sodium chicken broth
1/2	teaspoon salt

Char the chile by placing on a hot griddle. Heat until thoroughly blistered and charred. Use a pancake turner to exert pressure on the chile to char it evenly. When it is done, place in a damp, clean dish towel. This will loosen the skin for peeling. Carefully peel the charred skin and remove the veins and seeds. Set aside.

Remove the husks from the tomatillos. Wash thoroughly. In a large saucepan, boil them for approximately 5-10 minutes. Tomatillos are "done" when they have turned a dark green color and sink to the bottom of the pan. Remove from heat and drain using colander.

Use tongs to add tomatillos to a blender or food processor. Add all other ingredients and blend until smooth. Return mixture to saucepan. Cover, bring to a boil, reduce heat and simmer for one hour to allow flavors to blend.

<u>8 servings</u>

Nutrient Analysis: 1 serving
45 Calories, tr Fat, 1 g Fiber, 91 mg Sodium, tr Sat Fat, 0 mg Cholesterol
Diabetic Exchange: 1 VEGETABLE, 1/2 BREAD

SMOKED SALSA

Salsa Ahumada

2	pounds ripe red tomatoes
1/2	cup onions, chopped
2	garlic cloves, minced
1	teaspoon extra virgin olive oil
1/2	teaspoon oregano
1/2	teaspoon salt

Freshly ground pepper

After washing whole tomatoes, place them on a very hot griddle to char. The tomatoes must be turned frequently to char evenly on all sides. The process should take about 10-15 minutes. While tomatoes are charring, sauté onions and garlic in olive oil in a large skillet until onions are transparent. When tomatoes have charred evenly, combine with onions and garlic. Use a potato masher to crush tomatoes, onions and garlic until they reach desired consistency. Add seasonings and simmer gently for 15-20 minutes.

8 servings

Nutrient Analysis: 1 serving
31 Calories, 1 g Fat, 2 g Fiber, 143 mg Sodium, tr Sat Fat, 0 mg Cholesterol
Diabetic Exchange: 1/2 VEGETABLE

TOMATILLO SAUCE

Salsa de Tomatillo

This is another versatile salsa, but it is prepared with small green tomatoes called tomatillos. If the salsa is too "tart" a bit of sugar may be added to balance the flavor.

1 1/2   pounds tomatillos, peeled and rinsed in water
1/2   cup fresh cilantro
2   cloves fresh minced garlic
1   teaspoon salt
1/2   teaspoon pepper

Add cleaned tomatillos to 3-4 quarts water in a Dutch oven. Bring water to a rolling boil and boil tomatillos for 5-10 minutes, or until their color darkens and they begin to sink to bottom of pan.

Drain in colander. Use a fork or tongs to add tomatillos to blender or food processor along with cilantro, garlic, salt and pepper. Process until smooth.

May be frozen. Serve warm or cold.

Serves 8

Nutrient Analysis: 1 serving
21 Calories, 0 g Fat, 1 g Fiber, 278 mg Sodium, tr Sat Fat, 0 mg Cholesterol
Diabetic Exchange: 1 VEGETABLE

JICAMA TEXAS-STYLE

Jicama Tejano

1   **large jicama**
Juice of 3 limes
2   **teaspoons jalapeño powder (Texas gunpowder)**
       or red chili powder
1/2   teaspoon salt
Romaine lettuce

Wash and peel jicama, then slice into thin wedges. Place wedges in a large mixing bowl. Pour lime juice over all wedges, and gently toss to cover with lime juice. Set aside.

Mix jalapeño or chili powder and salt in a small, deep plate.

Take each wedge and dip inner edge into salt mixture and arrange in a circular fashion on a large platter lined with lettuce. Garnish with parsley or cilantro if desired.

<u>6 servings</u>

Nutrient Analysis: 1 serving
22 Calories, 0 g Fat, tr Fiber, 185 mg Sodium, 0 g Sat Fat, 0 mg Cholesterol
Diabetic Exchange: 1 VEGETABLE

SOUPS
&
BREADS

SOUPS AND BREADS

BEEF SOUP

Caldo de Res

This soup is loaded with Vitamin A!

1	pound very lean round steak, excess fat removed, cut into 1" cubes
2	quarts water
1/2	cup tomato sauce, no salt added
1/4	green pepper, cut in strips
1/2	onion, cut into strips
2	carrots, sliced in 1" pieces
1/2	head cabbage
2	potatoes, cut into fourths
2	ears fresh corn, cut into fourths
2	medium zucchini, cut into fourths
2	cloves garlic, ground
1	teaspoon salt
1/4	cup cilantro

In a Dutch oven sauté beef chunks until well browned. Drain any excess fat. Add 2 quarts water and bring to a boil. Reduce heat, add tomato sauce and vegetables. Grind garlic using molcajete. Use a small amount of water to loosen garlic from molcajete and pour into soup. Add salt and pepper, if desired.

Bring soup to a boil. Reduce heat, cover and simmer gently for 45 minutes. Add cilantro and simmer 15 minutes more.

Serves 4

Nutrient Analysis: 1 serving
324 Calories, 7 g Fat, 13 g Fiber, 668 mg Sodium, 2 g Sat Fat, 61 mg Cholesterol
Diabetic Exchange: 4 1/2 VEGETABLE, 2 BREAD, 3 MEAT, 1 FAT

MEATBALL SOUP

Sopa de Albondigas

The albondigas are lower in fat, and this soup also freezes well. It is excellent served with homemade corn tortillas on a chilly winter day.

Albondigas
1	**pound fresh, ground turkey breast**
1/4	**pound reduced-fat sausage**
1/2	**cup cooked rice**
1/4	**cup flour**
1/4	**cup water**
1	**teaspoon ground cumin**

Nonstick cooking spray
1	**large onion, cut in wedges**
3	**cloves garlic, minced or ground with cumin in molcajete**
1 1/2	**teaspoons freshly ground cumin seeds**
1	**tablespoon cilantro, chopped**
1	**14-ounce can pear-shaped tomatoes, chopped, reserve juice**
2 1/2	**quarts reduced-sodium beef broth**
2	**cups frozen corn, no salt added**
1	**fresh lime, cut in wedges**
1/2	**cup fresh cilantro, chopped**

Preheat oven to 450°.

In a large mixing bowl, combine turkey, sausage, rice, flour, cumin and water. Shape into meatballs, about 1 1/2 inches in size. Place on baking sheet. Bake at 450° until browned (about 30 minutes), turning occasionally to allow for even browning. Drain excess grease and set aside.

Spray a non-stick Dutch oven with cooking spray and sauté onions, garlic and cumin. Crush tomatoes and add together with juice to other ingredients. Add beef broth, corn and albondigas and simmer for 20 minutes.

Just before serving, top with fresh cilantro and serve with lime wedges and fresh corn tortillas.

<u>8 servings</u>

Nutrient Analysis: 1 serving
318 Calories, 11 g Fat, 3.5 gm Fiber, 1240 mg Sodium, 5.5 gm Sat Fat, 54 mg Cholesterol
Diabetic Exchange: 1 VEGETABLE, 1 BREAD, 3 1/2 MEAT, 1 1/2 FAT

TLALPEÑO SOUP

Caldo Tlalpeño

This soup is light and delicious, but it has a bite to it—because of the chipotle peppers!

8	cups lower-sodium chicken broth
1 1/4	pounds chicken breast fillet
1	onion, sliced
1	teaspoon vegetable oil
2	carrots, thinly sliced
1	medium zucchini, thinly sliced
2	cups yellow hominy
2	chipotle peppers canned in adobo
1	avocado, cut in chunks

Fresh limes, quartered

In a Dutch oven, bring chicken broth to a boil. Add chicken fillets and poach for 15 minutes. Remove fillets and shred chicken. Reserve broth. Strain if desired.

In a large nonstick pan, sauté onions in the vegetable oil. After onions have become translucent, add carrots and zucchini and saute until tender. Add sautéed vegetables, hominy and shredded chicken to chicken broth. Carefully cut chipotle peppers into strips and add to soup. Simmer gently 15-20 minutes.

Serve with avocado chunks and lime quarters.

Serves 8

Nutrient Analysis: 1 serving
210 Calories, 7 g Fat, 5 g Fiber, 1157 mg Sodium,1 g Sat Fat, 41 mg Cholesterol
Diabetic Exchange: 1 VEGETABLE, 1 BREAD, 3 1/2 MEAT, 1 FAT

GAZPACHO

This soup is flavorful and rich in vitamins. Although not Mexican in origin, it is enjoyed by many for its delicious flavor.

3	cups tomatoes, quartered
1	cucumber, peeled and chopped
1/2	cup onions, minced
2	tablespoons vinegar
1	tablespoon paprika
1	teaspoon salt
1/2	teaspoon pepper
1	drop Tabasco sauce
2	tablespoons cilantro, chopped
1 1/2	cups tomato juice

Add all ingredients except tomato juice to food processor or blender. Blend until smooth. Allow to chill 3-4 hours. Before serving, add 1 1/2 cups tomato juice.

Serve chilled, garnish with whole cilantro leaves.

Serves 4

Nutrient Analysis: 1 serving
73 Calories, 0 g Fat, 3 g Fiber, 1194 mg Sodium, tr Sat Fat, 0 mg Cholesterol
Diabetic Exchange: 2 1/2 VEGETABLE

* This recipe is very high in sodium. Reduce amount of sodium by using a no-salt tomato juice.

LENTIL SOUP

Sopa de Lentejas

Lentils are a good source of protein, and combined with corn tortillas they make a complete protein and a great "meatless" meal

1	tablespoon olive oil
1	small onion, chopped
1	stalk celery, chopped
1	carrot, peeled and chopped
1	cup lentils
1/4	cup dry red wine
3 1/2	cups water
1 1/2	teaspoon chili powder
1	bay leaf
1/2	teaspoon salt
1/4	teaspoon pepper
1/4	teaspoon allspice
1/2	teaspoon cumin
1	tomato, seeded and chopped
2	green onions, sliced diagonally (optional)

In a Dutch oven, heat olive oil, and add onions, celery and carrots. Sauté until tender. Add lentils and wine and heat to boiling. Cook over medium high heat until liquid is almost gone. Stir in water and spices. Heat to boiling. Decrease heat to low, cover and simmer 45 minutes. Stir in chopped tomato and cook 15 minutes more until lentils are tender. Garnish with onions if desired.

Serves 4

Nutrient Analysis: 1 serving
225 Calories, 4 g Fat, 8 g Fiber, 400 mg Sodium, 0 g Sat Fat, 0 mg Cholesterol
Diabetic Exchange: 2 VEGETABLE, 1 FAT

LENTILS

Lentejas

1	Anaheim chile pepper
1/2	cup minced green onions
2	cloves fresh garlic
1	14-ounce can whole tomatoes, no salt added, undrained, chopped
3/4	cup dried lentils
2	carrots, sliced thinly
1/2	teaspoon salt
1/2	teaspoon chili powder
3 1/4	cups beef broth
1/4	cup shredded lowfat Monterey Jack cheese

Wash lentils according to package directions and set aside.

Cut chile pepper in half lengthwise. Remove veins and seeds. Place chile, skin side up on baking sheet and press to flatten it. Broil in oven broiler for about 10 minutes, or until entire peel is blistered and charred. Immediately place pepper in a bowl with ice water. Chill 5 minutes. Remove from ice water and proceed to peel charred skin from chile. Chop chile and set aside.

In a Dutch oven, combine onions, garlic and undrained tomatoes. Heat thoroughly, stirring often. Add chopped chiles. Add lentils, salt, chile powder and beef broth. Bring to a boil. Cover and reduce heat. Simmer for about 45 minutes. Add carrots and simmer and additional 30-40 minutes, until lentils are tender. Serve topped with shredded cheese.

Serves 5

Nutrient Analysis: 1 serving
212 Calories, 5 g Fat, 7 g Fiber, 900 mg Sodium, 2.5 g Sat Fat, 12 mg Cholesterol
Diabetic Exchange: 2 VEGETABLE, 1 FAT

SEAFOOD SOUP

Sopa de Mariscos

Sopa de Mariscos is popular in South Texas. Different types of fish and sometimes shrimp are added to the soup for variation.

Nonfat cooking spray
1	**cup onion, chopped**
2	**medium tomatoes, seeded and chopped**
1/4	**cup green pepper, cut in strips**
3	**cloves garlic**
1/8	**teaspoon whole cumin**
2	**pounds snapper fillets, cut in 2" pieces**
1/4	**cup cilantro, chopped**
1	**teaspoon oregano, or to taste**
4	**tablespoons lime juice**
4	**cups water**
1/2	**teaspoon salt**
1/4	**teaspoon pepper**
2	**bay leaves**

Add cooking spray to a Dutch oven. Sauté the onions in the cooking spray. Add tomatoes and green peppers and sauté until tender. Grind garlic and cumin using molcajete, add water to loosen the spices. Add to vegetables.

Add all other ingredients and bring to a boil. Cover, lower heat and simmer for approximately one hour, stirring occasionally.

Remove bay leaves before serving. Serve with warm corn tortillas.

<u>Serves 4</u>

Nutrient Analysis: 1 serving
325 Calories, 6 g Fat, 4 g Fiber, 623 mg Sodium, 2 g Sat Fat, 62 mg Cholesterol
Diabetic Exchange: 1 VEGETABLE, 3 MEAT, 1/2 FAT

CHICKEN SOUP

Sopa de Pollo

2	pounds chicken breast, cut into strips
2	quarts water
2	cups canned tomatoes, crushed, no salt added
2	cloves garlic, minced
1	teaspoon cumin, ground
1	medium onion, cut wedges
1/4	teaspoon pepper
1	teaspoon salt
1/4	cup diced California green chiles
1/4	cup cilantro, if desired
2	cups hominy or cooked pinto beans, rinsed and drained
1	fresh lime

In a Dutch oven, cover chicken strips with about 2 quarts water. Cook until strips are tender. Remove chicken pieces from broth. Strain broth to remove foamy material.

Add tomatoes, garlic, cumin, onion, pepper, salt, chiles and chicken to broth. Add beans or hominy and simmer for 15 minutes.

Before serving, squeeze fresh lime juice over soup.

Serve with fresh corn tortillas.

Serves 6

Nutrient Analysis: 1 serving
253 Calories, 3.4 g Fat, 4 g Fiber, 678 mg Sodium, tr Sat Fat, 88 mg Cholesterol
Diabetic Exchange: 1 VEGETABLE, 1 BREAD, 4 MEAT

TORTILLA SOUP

Sopa de Tortillas

Don't let this recipe intimidate you. It is easy and very delicious!

2	medium tomatoes
Nonstick cooking spray	
1	cup onions, finely chopped
2	cloves garlic, minced or ground in molcajete
4	cups lower-sodium chicken broth
12	ounces chicken breast, cooked and cut into strips (about 2 chicken breasts, uncooked)
1/2	teaspoon pepper
8	corn tortillas, cut into strips and baked (see recipe page 96)
1/4	cup cilantro, stems removed, chopped

Heat broiler. Cut tomatoes in half and broil them until slightly charred, about 10-15 minutes, turning them occasionally to allow to heat evenly.

In a nonstick Dutch oven prepared with cooking spray, sauté onions. When tender, add minced or crushed garlic to onions and sauté together 2-3 minutes longer. In a food processor or blender, combine tomatoes, onions and garlic and blend until smooth.

Pour the puréed vegetables back into the Dutch oven. Add broth and chicken strips. Season with pepper. Bring to a boil. Cover, reduce heat and simmer for 20 minutes. Add cilantro and continue simmering for 10 more minutes. Serve immediately with baked tortilla chips arranged around bowl.

(This dish is usually served with lots of fried tortilla chips inside the soup. Since baked chips are being used, it is best they not be added to soup until ready to eat to prevent from getting soggy.)

<u>Serves 4</u>

Nutrient Analysis: 1 serving
315 Calories, 6 g Fat, 4 g Fiber, 1460 mg Sodium, 1 g Sat Fat, 66 mg Cholesterol
Diabetic Exchange: 1 VEGETABLE, 1 1/2 BREAD, 4 MEAT, 1/2 FAT

MEXICAN ROLLS

Bolillos

Bolillos are small French bread-like loaves. They are sometimes used in Mexico for sandwiches.

2   cups water
1 1/2   tablespoons sugar
1   tablespoon salt
2   tablespoons liquid margarine
1   package dry yeast
5 1/2 -6 cups all-purpose flour, divided
1   teaspoon cornstarch dissolved in 1 cup water
Nonstick cooking spray

Add water, sugar, salt and margarine to saucepan. Gently heat to bring to 115°. Use thermometer to assure proper temperature. Add yeast and stir well to dissolve.

Pour yeast liquid to a large mixing bowl. Add one cup of flour and beat well. Gradually add four more cups of flour, one cup at a time, stirring well after each addition.

Turn dough onto surface floured with remaining flour. Knead for 5 minutes or until dough is smooth and elastic.

Place dough in a large, lightly oiled bowl, turning once to oil surface. Cover with a damp cloth. Put in warm place to rise for 1 1/2 hours or until doubled in size.

Punch down and form into 16 oval-shaped loaves with tapered edges. Each loaf should be about 4 inches long.

Place on cookie sheets prepared with nonstick cooking spray.

Let rise for 35 minutes.

Preheat oven to 350°.

Heat cornstarch and water to boiling. Cool slightly. Brush each roll with mixture. Using a very sharp knife, make a deep slash down the middle of each roll.

Bake in 350° oven for 35-40 minutes, or until golden brown.

<u>16 servings</u>

Nutrient Analysis: 1 serving
190 Calories, 2 g Fat, 1 g Fiber, 414 mg Sodium, tr Sat Fat, 0 mg Cholesterol
Diabetic Exchange: 2 BREAD, 1/2 FAT

CORN TORTILLAS

Tortillas de Maiz

These are such a special treat, and really do not take very long to prepare. You do need corn flour (masa harina), a tortilla press, and preferably a large electric griddle that heats to at least 450°. A large griddle is better because it heats more evenly and can cook more tortillas at a time.

2 cups masa harina (corn flour)
1 teaspoon salt (optional)
1 to 1 1/4 cups lukewarm water
Nonstick cooking spray

Sift masa and salt together in a large bowl. Add one cup warm water and blend together using hands. Dough should become moistened and start to pull together. Add remaining water and work dough by hand until the bowl is clear of all dough. The masa should feel slightly moist and smooth. Form a large ball, then form small golf-sized balls. Allow dough balls to "rest" about 15 minutes in mixing bowl covered with a damp towel.

Heat griddle to 450°.

To prepare tortilla press, cut a piece of plastic wrap large enough to cover both sides of the press. Plastic should be folded in half with the folded edge placed against the hinge of the press.

Place a ball of masa in the bottom center of the tortilla press between the two plastic wrap sides.

Close the top part of the press and press lever down. The tortilla should be about 1/8" thick.

This may take a little practice!

If the tortilla is too thin, it may break when you transfer it to the griddle. If it is too thick, it may not cook properly.

The tortilla should be cooked on a hot griddle sprayed with nonstick cooking spray for about 2 minutes on one side. After two minutes, turn and cook on the other side for about 1 minute. Tortillas are done when the edges begin to lift and are a golden color.

<u>6 servings (2 tortillas)</u>

Nutrient Analysis: 1 serving
107 Calories, 1 g Fat, 0 g Fiber, tr mg Sodium, 0 g Sat Fat, 0 mg Cholesterol
Diabetic Exchange: 2 BREAD

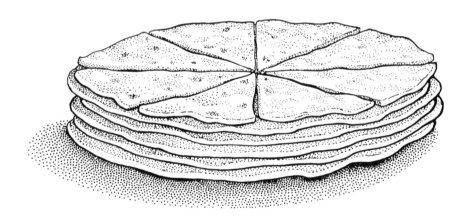

BAKED TORTILLA CHIPS

Tortillas Doradas

These are surprisingly good!

6   corn tortillas
Water
Lime juice, optional
1/2   teaspoon salt
Chili powder, optional
Nonstick cooking spray

Preheat oven to 500°. Using a sharp knife, cut tortillas into 6 wedge-shaped pieces. Pour 1/2 cup water into a pie plate. Dip tortilla wedges into water for 2-3 minutes, drain and place on cookie sheet that has been sprayed with nonstick cooking spray. Bake in 500° oven, checking often to make sure chips do not scorch — at this heat, foods tend to burn rapidly.

After approximately 5 minutes, remove cookie sheet from oven and turn each chip over to allow for even baking. At this time add lime juice and chile powder if desired or mix salt with chili powder. Spray chips with nonstick cooking spray to help salt or salt-chile mixture adhere to chips. Return to oven and bake for 2-3 minutes more. Eat warm or cold. Store in an airtight container.

<u>6 servings</u>

Nutrient Analysis: 1 serving
70 Calories, 1 g Fat, 1 g Fiber, 195 mg Sodium, tr Sat Fat, 0 mg Cholesterol
Diabetic Exchange: 1 BREAD

GARLIC PITA

Pita con Ajo

These are great with salsa or bean dip!

6	large whole wheat pita pocket breads
1/2	cup tub margarine, softened
2	tablespoons cilantro, minced finely
2	cloves minced garlic
1	teaspoon freshly squeezed lime juice
1/8	teaspoon lemon pepper (no salt)

Preheat oven to 450°.

With a serrated knife, cut each pita round into eight equal sections.

Combine margarine, cilantro, garlic and lime juice. Microwave ingredients for about 30 seconds to melt margarine, and stir to mix well.

Brush pita wedges with margarine mix. Sprinkle with lemon pepper.

Arrange on baking sheet and bake in 450° oven for 5 minutes, or until crisp and browned.

Serves 12

Nutrient Analysis: 1 serving
95 Calories, 4 g Fat, 2 g Fiber, 200 mg Sodium, tr Sat Fat, 0 mg Cholesterol
Diabetic Exchange: 1 BREAD, 1 1/2 FAT

CAMP BREAD

Pan de Campo

My grandfather was a real life Texas cowboy. While driving cattle through Texas, it was customary to bake "pan de campo" in a cast-iron skillet. This revised version is healthier than the original and very delicious!

2	**cups flour**
1	**tablespoon baking powder**
1/2	**tablespoon salt**
1/3	**cup oil**
2/3	**cup 2% milk**

Nonstick cooking spray

Preheat oven to 350°.

Prepare large cookie sheet by lightly spraying with nonstick cooking spray. Sift together dry ingredients. Add oil. Use pastry blender to make crumbly mixture. Add milk and work dough until it forms a ball. Dough may need a little additional flour. Remove from bowl and knead for about 2 minutes until smooth ball forms.

On a floured surface, use rolling pin to roll a circle about 11" in diameter and about 1/2 inch thick.

Place on prepared cookie sheet.

Bake in preheated oven for 25-30 minutes or until golden brown. Cut in 12 equal wedges and serve warm.

<u>Serves 12</u>

Nutrient Analysis: 1 serving
135 Calories, 6 g Fat, 0 mg Fiber, 374 mg Sodium,1 g Sat Fat, 1 mg Cholesterol
Diabetic Exchange: 1 BREAD, 1 1/2 FAT

TACO SHELLS

Tortillas para Tacos

Baked taco shells are lower in fat and calories than fried or store bought taco shells. Many purchased taco shells are prepared with tropical oils. These can be prepared ahead if needed.

1   recipe CORN TORTILLAS (page 96) made from corn flour (for 16 tortillas)
Nonstick cooking spray

Warm griddle to 450°.

Use tortilla press to make tortillas desired size.

Spray griddle with nonstick cooking spray. Cook one side of tortilla for two to three minutes and turn over. Cook other side of tortilla and gently fold tortilla edge to edge. Keep on griddle, turning to both sides and allowing to brown to a crispy texture.

6 servings (2 tortillas)

Nutrient Analysis: 1 serving
107 Calories, 1 g Fat, 0 mg Fiber, tr mg Sodium, 0 gm Sat Fat, 0 mg Cholesterol
Diabetic Exchange: 2 BREAD

MEXICAN ANISE BREAD

Semita

Anise has the wonderful aroma of licorice. This bread is good as a breakfast bread, dessert or "merienda," a Hispanic custom of a mid-afternoon coffee or tea with a Mexican pastry.

4-5	cups flour, divided
1	teaspoon salt
1	package dry yeast
1/4	cup sugar
1	cup anise tea*, cooled to 120°, unstrained
1/4	cup oil
2	egg whites
1	egg

Nonstick cooking spray

In a large bowl, sift together 2 cups flour, salt, yeast and sugar. Add warm anise tea to dry ingredients. Using mixer, mix for one minute at slow speed to blend. Then add oil, egg whites and egg, and beat for 3 minutes at high speed. Add remaining flour a little at a time and begin to knead to bring dough together. On a lightly floured surface, continue to knead dough for about 5 minutes until smooth ball forms.

Place dough in a bowl that has been lightly coated with oil. Turn dough over once to cover top surface with oil. Cover with damp cloth, and let rise in a warm place for one hour or until doubled.

After one hour, divide dough into 15 pieces. Form into small smooth dome-shaped "mounds," about 3 inches in diameter. Place on cookie sheet that has been sprayed with nonstick cooking spray.

Preheat oven to 375°. Allow bread to rise for 30 minutes. Bake for 17-18 minutes or until golden brown.

<u>Serves 15</u>

Nutrient Analysis: 1 serving
188 Calories, 4 g Fat, 1 g Fiber, 154 mg Sodium, 1 g Sat Fat, 18 mg Cholesterol
Diabetic Exchange: 2 BREAD, 1 FAT

* Prepare anise tea by boiling 1 1/2 teaspoons anise seed in water for 10-15 minutes. Strain, if desired. Anise may also be baked into the bread. Using this tea in the recipe will enhance the anise flavor in the bread.

WHOLE WHEAT PITA BREAD

Pan Pita de Trigo Integral

These are not Mexican, but they are very low in fat and great with Mexican, as well as other fillings. Don't let the yeast intimidate you; they are very easy to prepare and freeze well. Whole wheat pita bread is a great source of fiber and magnesium.

5-6	**cups whole wheat flour, divided**
1	**package active dry yeast**
2	**teaspoons salt**
2	**cups water, 120°**

Sift 2 cups flour, yeast and salt into a large mixing bowl. Gradually add water and beat until smooth. Add remaining flour a little at a time, working into a smooth ball. Knead for 5 minutes on a floured surface. Dough should be smooth and elastic.

Place dough in a large bowl that has been prepared with oil. Turn dough over once to cover top surface with oil, to prevent drying out. Cover bowl with damp cloth and put in a warm place to rise until doubled, about one hour. After one hour, punch dough down and let rest for 30 minutes covered with cloth.

Divide into 18 equal pieces and shape into balls.

Preheat oven to 450°.

On a floured surface, roll out each ball into a 5" diameter circle.

Place a cookie sheet in hot oven for 5 minutes to warm. Carefully remove cookie sheet and place dough circles on it.

Return to oven and bake for 5 to 6 minutes.

Bread will "puff" up while baking.

<u>Serves 18</u>

Nutrient Analysis: 1 serving
120 Calories, 1 g Fat, 4.5 g Fiber, 214 mg Sodium, tr Sat Fat, 0 mg Cholesterol
Diabetic Exchange: 2 BREAD, 1/2 FAT

WHOLE WHEAT TORTILLAS

Tortillas de Trigo Integral

1	cup whole wheat flour
1	cup white flour
2	teaspoons baking powder
1	teaspoon salt
3	tablespoons oil
1/2	cup boiling water, more if needed

Sift dry ingredients together. Add oil and work into dry ingredients using pastry blender until crumbly mixture is formed. Add boiling water and blend with pastry blender until cool enough to handle with hands. Use hands to knead dough 3 to 5 minutes or until smooth ball forms. Heat griddle to 450°.

Allow dough to rest for 20 minutes in covered bowl. This is very important.

Make 12 evenly formed balls from dough. Using rolling pin, roll each ball into a circle about 6" in diameter and 1/8" thick. It is best to roll all tortillas at the same time and save in between layers of plastic wrap or waxed paper if you don't plan to cook right away. Place each tortilla onto hot griddle, and cook for about four minutes on the first side and about three minutes on the second side. This will vary according to heating capabilities of griddle and even distribution of heat.

Save cooked tortillas in a tortilla warmer or covered dish.

Serves 6 (2 tortillas)

Nutrient Analysis: 1 serving
210 Calories, 7 g Fat, 3 g Fiber, 453 mg Sodium, 0 g Sat Fat, 0 mg Cholesterol
Diabetic Exchange: 2 BREAD 2 FAT

FLOUR TORTILLAS

Tortillas de Harina

3   cups flour
1   tablespoon baking powder
1   teaspoon salt
1/4   cup vegetable oil
1   cup boiling water

Blend together dry ingredients. Add vegetable oil to dry ingredients using pastry blender. Slowly add boiling water. Continue to blend with pastry blender until dough is workable with hands. By hand, form a ball and knead on a floured surface 3-5 minutes until smooth ball has formed.

Place in a bowl and cover with damp towel. Allow to "rest" for 20 minutes.

Heat griddle to 450°.

Form 18 balls from dough, and smooth into flattened balls. Using a rolling pin, roll each ball into a 6" circle about 1/8" thick.

Cook on hot griddle about 4 minutes on first side and about 3 minutes on second side. This will vary according to heating capabilities of griddle and even distribution of heat.

As tortillas cook, keep them warm and pliable in an insulated tortilla warmer or clean kitchen towel.

Serves 18

Nutrient Analysis: 1 serving
110 Calories, 3 g Fat, 1 g Fiber, 177 mg Sodium, tr Sat Fat, 0 mg Cholesterol
Diabetic Exchange: 1 BREAD 1/2 FAT

SALADS

SALADS

DRESSINGS

CABBAGE SALAD

Ensalada de Repollo

1/2	head cabbage, shredded
2	tomatoes, seeded and diced
1	cup onion, thinly sliced
2	stalks celery, chopped
1	cup jicama, in julienne strips
1/4	cup raisins
1	medium carrot, shredded
1/4	cup cilantro
4	slices avocado

Vinaigrette Dressing

1/4	cup lime juice
1/4	cup wine vinegar
2	tablespoons olive oil
1/8	teaspoon dry mustard

Mix ingredients for dressing. Set aside.

Toss cabbage and other vegetables except for avocado. Add dressing and toss gently again. Just before serving, add one slice of avocado to each serving.

Serves 4

Nutrient Analysis: 1 serving
168 Calories, 9 g Fat, 3.6 g Fiber, 34 mg Sodium, 1 g Sat Fat, 0 mg Cholesterol
Diabetic Exchange: 3 VEGETABLE, 2 FAT

CATALINA CABBAGE SALAD

Ensalada de Repollo Catalina

1	garlic clove, minced
1/4	cup apple cider vinegar
2	tablespoons salad oil
3	tablespoons nonfat Catalina dressing
2	tablespoons sugar
1/4	teaspoon pepper
3	cups cabbage, shredded
1/2	green pepper, chopped finely
2	large carrots, shredded

Combine first six ingredients in blender or food processor and blend until smooth.

Add to shredded vegetables and toss.

Refrigerate 3-4 hours to allow flavors to blend.

Serves 6

Nutrient Analysis: 1 serving
72 Calories, 2 g Fat, 2 g Fiber, 94 mg Sodium, tr g Sat Fat, 0 mg Cholesterol
Diabetic Exchange: 1 1/2 VEGETABLE, 1/2 FAT

CILANTRO CARROT SALAD

Ensalada Zanahoria con Cilantro

This salad is pretty and easy and a powerful source of natural beta carotene!

3   **cups carrots, peeled and cut in thin circles**
1/8   **cup cilantro, finely minced**
4   **tablespoons nonfat Catalina dressing**

Combine all ingredients. Refrigerate 1-2 hours before serving to allow flavors to blend.

Serves 6

Nutrient Analysis: 1 serving
56 Calories, tr Fat, 2.5 g Fiber, 117 mg Sodium, 0 g Sat Fat, 0 mg Cholesterol
Diabetic Exchange: 2 VEGETABLE

CILANTRO CUMIN VINAIGRETTE

Aderezo de Cilantro y Comino

Cumin seeds can be found in the spice section of the grocery store. Toasting these spicy little seeds before grinding will bring out a different flavor.

2   **tablespoons fresh squeezed lime juice**
2   **tablespoons olive oil**
1/2   **teaspoon cumin, toasted and ground**
1/2   **cup fresh cilantro, minced finely**
1   **clove garlic, minced**
1/8   **teaspoon salt**
Ground pepper

Add all ingredients to blender or food processor and process until all ingredients are well blended.

<u>Serves 4</u>

Nutrient Analysis: 1 serving
65 Calories, 7 g Fat, 0 g Fiber, 70 mg Sodium, 1 g Sat Fat, 0 mg Cholesterol
Diabetic Exchange: 1 FAT

CILANTRO DRESSING

Aderezo do Cilantro

2	**tablespoons fresh squeezed lime juice**
2	**tablespoons extra virgin olive oil**
1/8	**cup fresh cilantro, minced**
1	**clove garlic, minced**
1/8	**teaspoon salt**

Pepper, freshly ground

Add all ingredients to blender or mini-processor container. Blend well until a smooth consistency is achieved. Chill until ready to use. May be used as a dressing for lettuce or other fresh vegetable salad.

Serves 4

Nutrient Analysis: 1 serving
63 Calories, 7 g Fat, 0 g Fiber, 67 mg Sodium, 0 g Sat Fat, 0 mg Cholesterol
Diabetic Exchange: 1 1/2 FAT

CILANTRO MACARONI SALAD

Ensalada de Macaron con Cilantro

6	ounces nonfat plain yogurt
1/4	cup cilantro, stems removed
1	clove garlic
1	Serrano chile, stem and seeds removed
1/2	teaspoon salt
4	cups cooked macaroni
1/4	cup purple onion, chopped

Add yogurt, cilantro, garlic, chile and salt to blender or food processor. Blend for 45-60 seconds. Add to cooled macaroni and toss with onions. Refrigerate 3-4 hours to allow flavors to blend.

Serves 8

Nutrient Analysis: 1 serving
120 Calories, tr Fat, tr Fiber, 157 mg Sodium, 0 g Sat Fat, 1 mg Cholesterol
Diabetic Exchange: 1 BREAD

CILANTRO VINEGAR

Vinagre de Cilantro

This very low-calorie condiment is good on green salads and vegetables.

1   cup apple cider vinegar
1/2   cup fresh cilantro, stems removed
2   cloves garlic, crushed

Add vinegar, cilantro and garlic cloves to clean jar with tight fitting lid. Store in a dark place for 2 weeks.

Use on salads, meats and vegetables.

Serves 8

Nutrient Analysis: 1 serving
5 Calories, 0 g Fat, 0 g Fiber, 0 mg Sodium, 0 g Sat Fat, 0 mg Cholesterol
Diabetic Exchange: FREE

CILANTRO YOGURT DRESSING

Aderezo de Yogur y Cilantro

6	**ounces nonfat plain yogurt**
1/3	**cup cilantro, stems removed**
1	**clove garlic**
1	**Serrano chile**
1/2	**teaspoon salt**

Add all ingredients to blender or food processor. Blend until smooth. Refrigerate 3-4 hours to allow flavors to blend.

<u>Serves 6</u>

Nutrient Analysis: 1 serving
23 Calories, 0 g Fat, tr Fiber, 209 mg Sodium, 0 g Sat Fat, 0 mg Cholesterol
Diabetic Exchange: FREE

CUCUMBER TOMATO SALAD

Ensalada de Pepino y Tomate

2	**large cucumbers**
4	**small tomatoes**
2	**tablespoons fresh lime juice**

Freshly ground pepper
Lettuce leaves

Peel cucumbers, leaving about half of the peel on the cucumber for a striped effect. Remove ends of cucumbers and cut in disks. Wash and cut tomatoes in thin slices. Alternate cucumber disks and tomatoes on large flat platter lined with lettuce leaves. Squeeze fresh lime juice over vegetables. Dust lightly with freshly ground pepper.

<u>Serves 4</u>

Nutrient Analysis: 1 serving
45 Calories, 0 g Fat, 4 g Fiber, 13 mg Sodium, 0 g Sat Fat, 0 mg Cholesterol
Diabetic Exchange: 2 VEGETABLE

GARBANZO SALAD RIO GRANDE

Ensalada de Garbanzo Rio Grande

1	**14-ounce can garbanzos, rinsed and drained**
1	**tablespoon extra virgin olive oil**
1/4	**cup wine vinegar**
1	**clove garlic finely minced**
2	**tablespoons cilantro, chopped**
1/2	**cup purple onions, finely chopped**
1/4	**cup pimentos, drained**

Combine garbanzos in medium bowl with all remaining ingredients. Cover and refrigerate (stirring occasionally) for 2-3 hours or overnight.

<u>Serves 4</u>

Nutrient Analysis: 1 serving
210 Calories, 3.5 g Fat, 1 g Fiber, 224 mg Sodium, 1 g Sat Fat, 0 mg Cholesterol
Diabetic Exchange: 1 1/2 BREAD, 1 VEGETABLE, 1 FAT

JICAMA SALAD

Ensalada de Jicama

Jicama is a root-type vegetable that has a fresh, cool taste. It is commonly used in Southern California and Baja.

6	**tablespoons freshly squeezed lime juice**
1	**teaspoon sugar**
1/8	**teaspoon salt**
2	**large apples, cored and sliced in wedges**
1/2	**small jicama, peeled and rinsed**
1	**teaspoon chili powder, optional**

Leaf lettuce

About 20 minutes before serving, prepare round serving platter by lining with lettuce. In a large bowl, mix together lime juice, sugar and salt. Add apples and jicama. Toss gently to allow lime mixture to coat jicama and apples. Refrigerate until ready to serve. Just before serving, arrange on serving platter by alternating apples and jicama in a circle. Dust lightly with chili powder, if desired.

Serves 4

Nutrient Analysis: 1 serving
45 Calories, 0 g Fat, 1 g Fiber, 73 mg Sodium, 0 g Sat Fat, 0 mg Cholesterol
Diabetic Exchange: 1/2 VEGETABLE, 1/2 FRUIT

MEXICAN FIESTA SALAD

Ensalada Mejicana de Fiesta

1	head Romaine lettuce
2	tomatoes, seeded and cut into small pieces
1/2	cup green pepper, chopped finely
1	carrot, shredded
1	cup kidney beans, drained and rinsed
1/2	purple onion, sliced and separated into rings
1/2	cup nonfat Catalina dressing
1	avocado, sliced into small chunks

Prepare lettuce by tearing into bite-sized pieces. Gently toss lettuce, tomatoes, green pepper, carrots, beans and onions.

Just before serving, add dressing and toss again.

Arrange salad in individual serving bowls, and garnish with avocado chunks.

Serves 8

Nutrient Analysis: 1 serving
110 Calories, 4 g Fat, 3 g Fiber, 163 mg Sodium, tr Sat Fat, 0 mg Cholesterol
Diabetic Exchange: 1/2 BREAD, 1 VEGETABLE, 1 FAT

MEXICAN SPINACH SALAD

Ensalada de Espinacas Mejicana

This salad is rich in Vitamin A.

Dressing:
6   **ounces nonfat plain yogurt**
1/3   **cup cilantro, stems removed**
1   **clove garlic**
1   **Serrano chile**
1/4   **teaspoon salt**

Salad:
1   **10-ounce package fresh spinach, washed and patted dry**
4   **green onions, chopped**
1/2   **small jicama, peeled and cut into thin slices**
12   **cherry tomatoes, halved**

Add yogurt, cilantro, garlic, chile and salt to blender or food processor. Blend for 45-60 seconds.

Tear spinach into bite-sized pieces, and add to other vegetables in a large bowl. Toss gently.

Serve with cilantro yogurt dressing on the side.

<u>Serves 6</u>

Nutrient Analysis: 1 serving
50 Calories, tr Fat, 3 g Fiber, 250 mg Sodium, 0 g Sat Fat, 1 mg Cholesterol
Diabetic Exchange: 1 VEGETABLE

NOPALITO SALAD

Ensalada de Nopalito

Probably dating back to our Indian ancestors, many Hispanics enjoy eating nopalitos, young cactus leaves. My father-in-law fixes this interesting salad.

2	cups nopales, cleaned and cut in 1 inch pieces
1/2	cup onions, chopped
1	tomato, seeded and chopped
1/4	cup cilantro, chopped
1	teaspoon salt
1/2	teaspoon pepper
1	tablespoon fresh lime juice

Combine all ingredients and toss gently. Refrigerate 3-4 hours before serving.

Serves 4

Nutrient Analysis: 1 serving
40 Calories, 1 g Fat, 3 g Fiber, 272 mg Sodium, 0 g Sat Fat, 0 mg Cholesterol
Diabetic Exchange: 1 VEGETABLE

ONION AND TOMATO RELISH

Cebolla y Tomate

This is great with tacos, especially chorizo tacos.

3   **medium tomatoes, diced**
1   **small onion, chopped**
1/4   **cup apple cider vinegar**
1/2   **teaspoon salt**
1/4   **teaspoon pepper**

Toss vegetables with vinegar, salt and pepper.

Serves 4

Nutrient Analysis: 1 serving
22 Calories, tr Fat, 1 g Fiber, 183 mg Sodium, 0 g Sat Fat, 0 mg Cholesterol
Diabetic Exchange: 1 VEGETABLE

PINTO BEAN SALAD

Ensalada de Frijol Pinto

This is a great summer salad! Canned beans are firmer — rinse them in a colander to remove some of the sodium and starchy liquid.

2   **tablespoons extra virgin olive oil**
1/4 **cup cilantro, chopped**
1/4 **cup fresh lime juice**
4   **cups cooked pinto beans (firm) rinsed and drained**
1/2 **cup purple onion, chopped**
Lettuce leaves
2   **tomatoes, quartered**

In a small container with a lid, combine oil, cilantro and lime juice. Cover and shake to blend well. Set aside.

Add beans and onions to salad bowl. Toss with dressing. Chill 3-4 hours or overnight to allow flavors to blend.

Serve in individual salad bowls lined with lettuce leaves, and garnish with fresh tomato wedges.

<u>Serves 8</u>

Nutrient Analysis: 1 serving
110 Calories, 5 g Fat, 3 g Fiber, 115 mg Sodium, 1 g Sat Fat, 1 mg Cholesterol
Diabetic Exchange: 1 1/2 BREAD, 1 FAT

ENTREES

ENTREES

A NOTE ON ENCHILADAS

The enchilada is Mexican dish in which a softened tortilla, usually corn, is wrapped around meat, cheese, vegetables, or a combination of all three. The rolled tortilla is then covered with a sauce such as a red chili or tomato sauce.

Typically, when preparing the enchilada, the tortilla is fried to soften it before filling but this adds many unnecessary calories. An alternative method for softening tortillas is to moisten a clean kitchen towel with water, wrap tortillas and microwave. This steams the tortillas and softens them for filling and rolling.

To make enchiladas lower in fat and calories, try preparing a vegetable filling combined with a lower-fat cheese. Alternatively, using a lower-fat meat such as turkey, chicken or lean ground beef will also decrease fat calories.

There are many wonderful low-fat sauces available for the preparation of enchiladas. TOMATILLO SAUCE (page 78), for example, is high in Vitamin C and very low in fat. FAT-FREE RED CHILI SAUCE (page 69) is also perfect for a lower-fat enchilada.

While they are typically a rich, high-fat food, enchiladas can be made healthier. Try the three delicious recipes listed in this section!

A NOTE ON TAMALES

In many Hispanic households, the arrival of cooler weather and impending holidays prompts the desire to eat tamales. They are an essential part of traditional Mexican food prepared for Christmas and the New Year.

The tamale has been a part of Mexican cuisine dating back to Indian ancestors. When the Spanish conquistadors arrived in the New World in the 1500's, native people ate tamales to celebrate special occasions. Four hundred years later, the traditions of our ancestors are continued.

In the Mexican-American culture, the *tamalada* has come to be a time when generations gather to help in this traditional food preparation. Experienced grandmothers offer their advice on the numerous preparations for which few recipes actually exist. Each family has its own "heirloom recipe."

There exists a hierarchy as the younger members of the family are assigned the more menial tasks such as soaking and cleaning corn shucks. The more experienced cook prepares the ingredients. He or she is also likely to *embarar* or carefully line the corn shuck with masa (prepared corn dough). In the ancient custom of utilizing all gifts from nature, corn shucks were and still are used for wrapping and cooking the tamales.

Different regions of the Southwest have different ways of preparing the tamale. In California, the tamale is large and may have either meat or fruit fillings. In Arizona, one version of the tamale is made with cheese and chiles. The Texas tamale is a bit smaller and usually made only with meat or beans. In some areas where deer hunting is a sport, tamales are made using venison or a combination of highly spiced venison and pork or beef.

Another version of the tamale involves combining this highly spiced meat with raisins, giving tamales a spicy sweet flavor. A special treat is the corn tamale, made entirely with fresh ground corn kernels, usually prepared in the summer as corn is being harvested from the fields.

Technology has changed considerably from the days when Indians hand ground their maize. Food processors and machine-processed corn flour are now common in the Mexican-American kitchen. In spite of technology, an important ancient tradition is carried on. Women and men gather to prepare this food, to laugh, talk and strengthen the weaves of family ties.

Despite the time and effort involved, tamales continue to be a strong tradition for the Mexican-American family. This section contains complete directions on making healthier versions of these delicious tamales, in several tempting variations.

BREAKFAST PITAS

Pita de Desayuno

2	whole wheat pita breads, halved
8	ounces lowfat Mozzarella cheese
1/2	cup TOMATILLO SAUCE, warmed (page 78)

Cut pita bread in halves and warm slightly by toasting or microwaving. Open each pocket, and add cheese and tomatillo sauce. Warm again until cheese melts slightly.

Serves 4

Nutrient Analysis: 1 serving
190 Calories, 6 g Fat, 3 g Fiber, 826 mg Sodium, tr Sat Fat, 10 mg Cholesterol
Diabetic Exchange: 1 BREAD, 2 MEAT, 1/2 FAT

CHALUPAS

3   **cups cooked low-fat pinto beans**
2   **ounces Monterey Jack cheese, shredded**
2   **ounces lowfat Cheddar cheese, shredded**
1   **cup lettuce, shredded**
1   **large tomato, seeded and chopped**
3   **green onions, chopped**
12   **corn tortillas**
Nonfat cooking spray

Preheat oven to 500°.

Prepare beans by mashing in a large skillet. Slowly cook until most of the liquid has evaporated and beans thicken. Keep beans warm until ready to assemble chalupas. Do not allow them to become too dry.

Bake whole tortillas by first dipping them in cold water briefly and arranging on a cookie sheet that has been sprayed with nonfat cooking spray.

Heat in 500° oven for 5 minutes. Remove from oven, turn and heat for 3-4 more minutes, watching carefully so tortillas do not scorch. Foods tend to burn easily at this heat. Reduce heat to 350°. Spread thickened beans on tostada shells. Top with cheese and return to 350° oven. Bake until cheese melts.

Add lettuce, tomatoes and green onions before serving.

<u>Serves 6</u>

Nutrient Analysis: 1 serving
350 Calories, 7 g Fat, 6 g Fiber, 336 mg Sodium, 2.8 g Sat Fat , 12 mg Cholesterol
Diabetic Exchange: 3 BREAD, 1 MEAT, 1 FAT

MUSHROOM ENCHILADAS

Enchiladas de Hongos

These are a higher fat food, but delicious for a special treat.

1	recipe **RED CHILI SAUCE (page 73)**
8	**cups fresh mushrooms, sliced**
12	**corn tortillas**
6	**1-ounce servings string cheese (part skim Mozzarella cheese)**

Nonstick cooking spray

Prepare chile sauce and set aside.

In a large pan coated with nonstick cooking spray, sauté mushrooms until tender.

Steam tortillas, two at a time in microwave. This may be done by placing tortillas in a dampened kitchen towel and microwaving for about two minutes, being careful when removing them from oven.

Preheat oven to 350°. Add a small amount of chile sauce to bottom of large baking pan. Leave remaining sauce in frying pan and dip each tortilla in sauce until well coated. Lay tortilla flat on a plate or cutting board. Add 1/2 strip of cheese and some mushrooms to the middle of a tortilla and roll up, placing seam side down in baking pan. Repeat with other tortillas. Pour remaining sauce over enchiladas.

Heat in 350° oven for 15-20 minutes or until cheese melts.

Serves 6

Nutrient Analysis: 1 serving
325 Calories, 15 g Fat, 6 g Fiber, 490 mg Sodium, 4 g Sat Fat, 16 mg Cholesterol
Diabetic Exchange: 1 BREAD, 1 VEGETABLE, 1 MEAT, 1 1/2 FAT

RED CHILI ENCHILADAS

Enchiladas de Chile Colorado

1	recipe RED CHILI SAUCE (page 73)
10	corn tortillas
10	ounces lowfat Cheddar cheese, shredded
1/2	cup onions, chopped finely

Preheat oven to 350°

Wrap 2 tortillas in a clean, dampened kitchen towel. Steam in microwave for 2 1/2 minutes or until steamed thoroughly. Remove carefully from microwave and fill each with some cheese and onions. Roll and place seam side down in baking dish. Repeat process with remaining tortillas and ingredients. Cover with red chili sauce and heat in oven for about 20 minutes, or until cheese melts.

<u>Serves 5</u>

Nutrient Analysis: 1 serving
400 Calories, 21 g Fat, 2 g Fiber, 879 mg Sodium, 5 g Sat Fat, 30 mg Cholesterol
Diabetic Exchange: 2 BREAD, 2 MEAT, 1/2 VEGETABLE, 3 FAT

TORTAS

This breakfast dish is usually made with bolillos—small loaves of bread similar to French bread.

1/2	loaf French bread, cut into 12 slices or 6 small **BOLILLOS** (page 94), sliced in half lengthwise
2	cups **UNFRIED REFRIED BEANS** warmed (page 203)
1/2	cup lowfat Monterey Jack cheese, shredded
1/2	cup lowfat Cheddar cheese, shredded

Toast French bread slices or bolillo halves.

Preheat oven to 350°. Spread beans over bread. Mix the two lowfat cheeses and add to top of beans and bread. Bake in 350° oven until thoroughly warmed and cheese has melted.

Serve with fresh salsa.

<u>Serves 6</u>

Nutrient Analysis: 1 serving
300 Calories, 9 g Fat, 4 g Fiber, 555 mg Sodium, 5 g Sat Fat, 22 mg Cholesterol
Diabetic Exchange: 2 BREAD, 1 MEAT, 2 FAT

COD STEAKS MEXICANA

Bacalao Mejicana

1	teaspoon oil
1	green pepper, seeded and sliced
1	red pepper, seeded and sliced
1	large onion, sliced in strips
2	cloves garlic, ground
1/2	teaspoon cumin seeds, ground
1/4	teaspoon salt
1/4	teaspoon pepper
4	cod fillets, about 4 ounces each

In a large nonstick skillet with a lid, heat oil. Over medium heat, sauté all vegetables along with garlic, cumin, salt and pepper that have been ground in molcajete. Stir frequently to cook vegetables evenly.

Remove from pan and set aside.

Rinse fish and place in skillet. Rearrange vegetables on top of fish. Cover and cook until fish is opaque and flaky, about 15 minutes.

Serves 4

Nutrient Analysis: 1 serving
110 Calories, 2 g Fat, 1 g Fiber, 615 mg Sodium, tr Sat Fat, 56 mg Cholesterol
Diabetic Exchange: 1 VEGETABLE, 3 MEAT

FISH IN SALSA

Pescado en Salsa

Some of the better fish choices include albacore tuna, red salmon and sardines. These are rich in fish oils which some research has shown to be effective in the prevention of heart disease. This recipe is especially good when made with smoked salsa, and it is best to use a firm fish to prepare this dish.

**2   pounds firm fish fillets, skinned,
cut in serving sizes**

**2   cups MORNING SAUCE (page 71)
or other favorite salsa**

Add salsa to large skillet with tight-fitting lid. Heat until salsa begins to boil. Place fish fillets on top of salsa. Cover with lid and simmer about 10 minutes or until fish flakes with a fork.

Carefully transfer to serving platter. Serve with extra salsa.

Serves 8

Nutrient Analysis: 1 serving
150 Calories, 2.4 g Fat, 0 mg Fiber, 626 mg Sodium, tr Sat Fat, 62 mg Cholesterol
Diabetic Exchange: 1/2 VEGETABLE, 4 MEAT

GRILLED SALMON CHIPOTLE

Salmon Parrillado con Chipotle

Chipotles are tasty smoked jalapenos canned in tomato sauce and can be found in the Hispanic section of the grocery store. Purchase salmon steaks that are not too thick, for quicker grilling time.

2   4-ounce salmon steaks about 1" thick
Juice of one lime
1/2   cup tomato sauce, no salt added
1   chipotle pepper with sauce

Marinate salmon steaks in lime juice for 2 hours.

Prepare salsa by adding tomato sauce and chipotle pepper to blender or food processor. Puree until smooth. Set aside.

Cook salmon steaks over glowing coals, 7 to 8 minutes on either side until fish is cooked.

Serve hot with salsa.

Serves 2

Nutrient Analysis: 1 serving
150 Calories, 4 g Fat, 1 g Fiber, 78 mg Sodium, 1 g Sat Fat, 40 mg Cholesterol
Diabetic Exchange: 1/2 VEGETABLE, 4 MEAT

GULF FISH AND WILD RICE

Pescado del Golfo con Arroz

1	pound flounder fillets (or other fish), cut into 1" squares
1	cup onions, chopped
1	tablespoon tub margarine
4	cups cooked brown rice, warm
1/2	cup diced green chiles, drained
1/2	cup diced pimientos
1	teaspoon salt

Nonstick cooking spray
Lowfat sour cream, optional

Preheat oven to 350°.

Poach fish chunks in large skillet. Drain and set aside. Sauté onions, chiles and pimientos in the margarine until tender. Spray 2-quart casserole dish with nonstick cooking spray. Add rice, green chiles, pimientos, salt and poached fish and toss gently until well mixed. Bake in 350° oven for 15-20 minutes or until thoroughly warmed. Top with lowfat sour cream, if desired. Serve with salad.

Serves 4

Nutrient Analysis: 1 serving
361 Calories, 4.5 g Fat, 3 g Fiber, 665 mg Sodium, 1 g Sat Fat, 56 mg Cholesterol
Diabetic Exchange: 1 1/2 BREAD, 4 MEAT, 1/2 VEGETABLE, 1 FAT

SALMON PATTIES

Albondigas de Salmon

Salmon and fish patties are foods used by many Hispanics during Lent. This version incorporates red salmon, a fatty fish rich in Omega-3 fatty acids, which are supposed to help prevent heart disease. These patties are also a great source of calcium.

1	**7.75-ounce can red salmon**
2	**tablespoons flour**
1/4	**cup egg substitute**
1	**teaspoon oil**

Mix salmon, flour and egg substitute until well blended. Form four patties from mixture. Patties will not hold their shape well at this point, but after cooking, they will be firm.

Heat oil in large nonstick frying pan. Using pancake turner, transfer patties into hot oil. Cook each side until it appears golden brown.

<u>Serves 2</u>

Nutrient Analysis: 1 serving
246 Calories, 9 g Fat, .2 g Fiber, 560 mg Sodium, 2 g Sat Fat, 41 mg Cholesterol
Diabetic Exchange: 1/2 BREAD, 3 MEAT, 1/2 FAT

SNAPPER VERDE

Huachinango Verde

2   pounds snapper fillets
1/2   teaspoon salt
Pepper, to taste
2   limes, peeled and sliced thinly
2   teaspoons olive oil
1   cup TOMATILLO SAUCE (page 78)

Line cookie sheet with foil. Place fish on foil. Sprinkle each fillet with salt and pepper. Place slices of lime on each fillet. Cover pan with foil and refrigerate 4-5 hours.

Preheat oven to 450°. Remove fish from refrigerator and brush each fillet with olive oil. Bake for 30 minutes or until flesh turns whitish and flakes easily.

Serve immediately with warmed TOMATILLO SAUCE.

<u>Serves 8</u>

Nutrient Analysis: 1 serving
123 Calories, 2 g Fat, 0 g Fiber, 215 mg Sodium, tr Sat Fat, 62 mg Cholesterol
Diabetic Exchange: 3 MEAT

SWORDFISH STEAKS WITH SALSA

Pez Espada con Salsa Casera

This is so delicious and easy to fix. Serve with ARROZ CON LIMA (page 199) and a salad for a special dinner.

4	**swordfish steaks, approximately 4 ounces each**
1	**tablespoon oil**
2	**cloves garlic, crushed in molcajete**
1/2	**cup onions, chopped**
1	**jalapeno, seeded and minced finely**
5	**tomatoes, firm, seeded and chopped**
1	**tablespoon fresh lime juice**
1/2	**cup cilantro, chopped, stems removed**

Rinse fish. Heat oil in a large skillet using medium high heat. Sauté garlic and onions and remove from skillet. Add fish steaks and sauté until well browned. The swordfish flesh should become white in the center and should flake easily. Cooking time is about 5 minutes. Remove from skillet and keep warm.

Add jalapeño to skillet with onions and garlic and sauté again. Add tomatoes, lime juice and cilantro and continue to sauté all vegetables about 5 minutes, stirring frequently. Spoon over warmed fish.

Serve immediately.

<u>Serves 4</u>

Nutrient Analysis: 1 serving
207 Calories, 8 g Fat, 3 g Fiber, 75 mg Sodium,2 g Sat Fat, 62 mg Cholesterol
Diabetic Exchange: 4 MEAT, 1 1/2 VEGETABLE, 1 FAT

CHICKEN FIESTA

Pollo Fiesta

Nonstick cooking spray
1/2   cup sliced green onions
2   cups sliced fresh mushrooms
1/2   cup diced green chiles, drained
1/4   cup cilantro, chopped
1 1/2 cups MORNING SAUCE (page 71) or other salsa
1   pound cooked chicken breasts, shredded
2   cups brown rice, cooked
1   cup lowfat plain yogurt
4   ounces grated Cheddar cheese
Paprika
Green Onions

Spray nonstick skillet with cooking spray and heat. Add onions, mushrooms, chiles and cilantro. Cook 4-5 minutes, then stir in salsa and cook until most liquid has evaporated.

Preheat oven to 350°. Spray 2-quart baking dish with cooking spray. Reserve 1/2 cup of cooked vegetable mixture and add the rest with the shredded chicken.

Mix together rice, yogurt and reserved vegetables, then combine both mixtures and pour into casserole dish. Top with cheese, paprika and green onions. Bake 35-40 minutes or until thoroughly warmed.

Serves 6

Nutrient Analysis: 1 serving
340 Calories, 7 g Fat, 3 g Fiber, 500 mg Sodium, 6 g Sat Fat, 80 mg Cholesterol
Diabetic Exchange: 1 BREAD, 4 MEAT, 1/2 VEGETABLE, 1 FAT

CHICKEN AND VEGETABLES

Pollo con Verduras

1	pound chicken breast fillets, skinned

Nonstick cooking spray

1	medium onion, sliced
2	large tomatoes, chopped
3	cloves garlic
1/2	teaspoon freshly ground cumin
4	whole peppercorns
2	tablespoons vinegar
1	head cabbage, cut into eighths
12	ounces frozen, whole-kernel corn, no salt added

Cut chicken breast into small strips. Spray the bottom of Dutch oven with cooking spray. Add chicken strips and sauté.

Add the onions and tomatoes, sautéing all together for 2-3 minutes.

In a blender, combine garlic and spices with vinegar. Add to the chicken and vegetables and mix well. Add the cabbage and corn. Cover.

Cook for 25-30 minutes or until cabbage is tender.

<u>Serves 4</u>

Nutrient Analysis: 1 serving
335 Calories, 10 g Fat, 5 g Fiber, 370 mg Sodium, 2.5 g Sat Fat, 86 mg Cholesterol
Diabetic Exchange: 1 BREAD, 3 1/2 MEAT, 2 VEGETABLE

CHICKEN ADOBO

Pollo Adobado

2	pounds chicken breasts, skinned, cut in pieces
1	cup chopped onions
1/2	cup low-sodium chicken broth
3	tablespoons red chili powder
2	garlic cloves
1	tablespoon red wine vinegar
1/2	teaspoon oregano, Mexican if possible
1/2	teaspoon freshly ground cumin
1/2	teaspoon salt
12	corn tortillas
1/2	cup green onions, chopped finely

Purée all ingredients except chicken, tortillas and green onions in blender container. Pour half of the chile puree into a large baking dish with a cover. Arrange chicken pieces in the dish and pour remaining chili mixture over the chicken. Cover and refrigerate overnight. Remove from refrigerator about 30 minutes before baking.

Preheat oven to 350°. Bake covered chicken for 30 minutes. Remove cover and bake 45 minutes more, basting occasionally with chile sauce.

Shred chicken. Remove any fat from sauce. Return to pan and bake 15 minutes longer. Serve on warm corn tortillas with chopped green onions.

Serves 6

Nutrient Analysis: 1 serving
322 Calories, 4.7 g Fat, 3 g Fiber, 400 mg Sodium, 1 g Sat Fat, 88 mg Cholesterol
Diabetic Exchange: 2 BREAD, 3 MEAT, 1/2 VEGETABLE, 1/2 FAT

CHICKEN CILANTRO

Pollo en Cilantro

Serve with THE BEST MEXICAN RICE (page 192) and fresh corn tortillas.

1 1/2	**pounds chicken breast fillets, cooked and shredded**
1 1/2	**pounds tomatillos**
2	**cloves garlic**
1	**teaspoon salt**
1/2	**teaspoon pepper**
1	**cup cilantro, washed and chopped, large stems removed**
1/2	**teaspoon olive oil**
1	**large onion, chopped finely**

Remove outer layer from tomatillos. Rinse well in warm water to remove all dirt and debris. Add to Dutch oven with 3-4 quarts warm water. Bring to a boil. Continue boiling tomatillos until skin has turned brownish green and has broken slightly, about 10 minutes.

Pour into colander to remove all excess water. Using fork or thongs, add warm tomatillos to blender or food processor container and blend with garlic, salt, pepper and cilantro until mixture becomes a smooth sauce. Set aside.

Add oil to nonstick skillet and sauté chopped onions until tender. Add shredded chicken and blended tomatillo cilantro sauce. Simmer slowly uncovered for 30 minutes.

<u>Serves 6</u>

Nutrient Analysis: 1 serving
185 Calories, 2 g Fat, 3 g Fiber, 445 mg Sodium, 1 g Sat Fat, 66 mg Cholesterol
Diabetic Exchange: 4 MEAT, 2 VEGETABLE

SAUCY CHICKEN

Pollo Guisado

This is an adaptation of one of my mother's recipes. My children all tested it and gave it rave reviews.

1 1/2   **pounds chicken breast fillets, cut into 1" cubes**
2   **garlic cloves, ground**
1   **teaspoon cumin, freshly ground**
1/4   **teaspoon whole black pepper, freshly ground (less if desired)**
2   **cups water**
2   **tablespoons tomato sauce**
1/2   **teaspoon salt**
2   **tablespoons flour**
Nonstick cooking spray

Spray a Dutch oven with nonstick cooking spray. Brown chicken cubes using medium heat. Grind garlic, pepper and cumin in molcajete. Use small amount of water to loosen spices and add to chicken. Add tomato sauce and salt. Bring to a boil, reduce heat, cover and simmer for 10 minutes.

Dissolve flour in two cups water to make a smooth liquid. Add to chicken, stirring frequently to allow gravy to thicken.

Bring to a boil, reduce heat and simmer for 15 minutes more.

Serves 6

Nutrient Analysis: 1 serving
140 Calories, 1.5 g Fat, 0 g Fiber, 282 mg Sodium, tr Sat Fat, 66 mg Cholesterol
Diabetic Exchange: 3 1/2 MEAT

CHICKEN POSOLE

Posole con Pollo

This is a good substitute for menudo, a red chili stew made from tripe. This recipe is lower in cholesterol and fat and tastes great.

1	medium onion, chopped
2	cloves garlic, minced
1 1/4	pounds cooked chicken breast, cut in strips
1/4	pound cooked lean pork tenderloin, cut in strips
6	cups hominy, drained and rinsed
8	cups water
2	tablespoons ground chili powder
1	teaspoon salt
1/4	teaspoon oregano, optional

Nonstick cooking spray
Radishes, sliced thinly
Cilantro, chopped
Lime wedges

In a Dutch oven, sauté onion and garlic using cooking spray. Add chicken and pork pieces. Cook until meats are thoroughly browned. Add water, chili powder, hominy, salt and oregano. Bring to a boil, cover and simmer for 20-30 minutes. Serve with radishes, cilantro, lime wedges and warm tortillas.

Serves 6

Nutrient Analysis: 1 serving
315 Calories, 6.5 g Fat, 10 g Fiber, 744 mg Sodium, 1.5 g Sat Fat, 70 mg Cholesterol
Diabetic Exchange: 2 BREAD, 4 MEAT, 1/2 VEGETABLE

ORANGE CHICKEN

good

Pollo con Naranja

1	6-ounce can frozen orange juice concentrate
2	cloves garlic
1/2	teaspoon pepper
1/2	teaspoon cumin seeds
1/2	teaspoon red chili powder
1	small jalapeño, seeded and diced
1	teaspoon salt
1 1/2	pounds chicken breast, skinned
1/2	cup onions, cut in strips
8	small red potatoes, scrubbed and cut in quarters

1 can pineapple   2-3 tbls brown sugar

~~Set crock pot to high.~~

Brown chicken in oil in skillet

Add orange juice, garlic, pepper, cumin, red chili powder, jalapeño and salt to ~~blender or food processor and blend until smooth.~~ pan

Place chicken breasts in crock pot and pour orange juice mixture over chicken. Top with onions and potatoes.

Cook for 6 hours on high. Internal chicken temperature should reach 160° before serving.

<u>Serves 4</u>

Nutrient Analysis: 1 serving
465 Calories, 3 g Fat, 5 g Fiber, 658 mg Sodium, 1 g Sat Fat, 98 mg Cholesterol
Diabetic Exchange: 1 1/2 BREAD, 5 MEAT, 1/2 VEGETABLE, 1 FRUIT

CHICKEN AND RICE

Arroz con Pollo

1 1/2 pounds chicken breast fillets, cut in strips
1   teaspoon oil
1 1/2 cups long grain rice
2   tablespoons finely chopped onions
3   cups lower-sodium chicken broth
1   cup stewed tomatoes, crushed
1/2   teaspoon salt
2   cloves garlic
1/4   teaspoon whole black pepper
1/4   teaspoon cumin
1   cup frozen peas and carrots
Nonstick cooking spray

In a large skillet, using a small amount of nonstick cooking spray, brown chicken. Remove from pan.

Add one teaspoon oil to pan. Sauté rice and onions, stirring frequently until rice has turned opaque and a light brown color. Add chicken broth, undrained crushed tomatoes and salt. Grind garlic, pepper and cumin in molcajete. Add a small amount of water to molcajete to loosen spices. Add to rice. Bring mixture to boiling, stirring well.

Arrange chicken pieces on top of rice mixture. Cover, reduce heat and steam for 25-30 minutes. After 25 minutes, add peas and carrots, cover and heat for 5 more minutes.

<u>Serves 6</u>

Nutrient Analysis: 1 serving
335 Calories, 3 g Fat, 2 g Fiber, 726 mg Sodium, 1 g Sat Fat, 65 mg Cholesterol
Diabetic Exchange: 2 1/2 BREAD, 3 1/2 MEAT, 1/2 VEGETABLE, 1/4 FAT

CHICKEN AND SQUASH

Calabaza con Pollo

Rich in Vitamin C and very low in fat, this dish is prepared using Tatuma squash, a round green summer squash.

1	pound chicken breast fillets, skinned
Nonstick cooking spray	
8	cups Mexican (Tatuma) squash, cut into 1-inch pieces, peeled if desired
1/2	cup onion
1	cup frozen corn kernels
1/2	teaspoon cumin seed
1/8	teaspoon whole black pepper
2	large cloves garlic
2	tablespoons water
1/4	teaspoon salt
1/3	cup stewed tomatoes

Cut chicken fillets into small pieces and add to warmed Dutch oven that has been coated with cooking spray. Heat gently over medium heat. Brown, stirring often. Sauté about 10 minutes. Add squash and onion. Allow to cook along with chicken for another 10 minutes. Add corn and stir together.

In molcajete, grind cumin, black pepper and garlic. Add water to loosen spices and add to chicken and vegetables. Add salt and stewed tomatoes, and stir to blend. Cover and simmer for 15-20 minutes or until squash is tender, stirring occasionally. Serve with corn tortillas and fresh pinto beans.

Serves 4

Nutrient Analysis: 1 serving
200 Calories, 2 g Fat, 6 g Fiber, 320 mg Sodium, 1 g Sat Fat, 50 mg Cholesterol
Diabetic Exchange: 1/2 BREAD, 3 MEAT, 3 VEGETABLE

CHICKEN TACO SALAD

Ensalada de Pollo

1	**pound cooked chicken breast fillets, cut into strips**
1	**cup PICO DE GALLO (page 72) or other salsa**
16	**baked tortilla chips (four corn tortillas)**
	or 4 ounces commercially baked chips
4	**cups shredded Romaine lettuce**
1/2	**purple onion, sliced and cut into rings**
1	**tomato, seeded and chopped**
1	**15-ounce can kidney beans, rinsed and drained**
1/2	**cup lowfat Cheddar cheese, shredded**

Nonstick cooking spray

Coat a large nonstick skillet with cooking spray. Heat chicken strips slightly, then add PICO DE GALLO or other salsa. Cover and simmer 8-10 minutes on low heat. Shred chicken with fork then cool in refrigerator. To serve, arrange a layer of baked tortilla chips, top with shredded lettuce. Add chopped tomatoes and onions and place shredded chicken on top. Garnish with shredded cheese and kidney beans.

Serves 4

Nutrient Analysis: 1 serving
470 Calories, 13 g Fat, 5 g Fiber, 440 mg Sodium, 4 g Sat Fat, 115 mg Cholesterol
Diabetic Exchange: 2 BREAD, 5 MEAT, 1 VEGETABLE, 2 FAT

SOUTHWESTERN CHICKEN

Pollo Suroeste

1 1/2 pounds chicken breasts (or 6 fillets), stewed
3   cups MORNING SAUCE (page 71)

Warm MORNING SAUCE in a large nonstick skillet with a lid. Add chicken breast fillets. Cover with lid and heat for 15-20 minutes until fully heated. Serve chicken breast with sauce.

Serve with JALAPEÑO RICE (page 198) and green salad.

<u>Serves 6</u>

Nutrient Analysis: 1 serving
175 Calories, 3 g Fat, 2 g Fiber, 278 mg Sodium, 1 g Sat Fat, 73 mg Cholesterol
Diabetic Exchange: 3 MEAT, 1 VEGETABLE

KING RANCH CHICKEN

Pollo King Ranch

This recipe is a Texas favorite named after the famous King Ranch. This version is much lower in fat and sodium than the original and makes a wonderful meal served with a salad.

1	**pound cooked chicken breast, shredded**
12	**corn tortillas**
1	**cup fat-free Cheddar cheese, shredded**
1	**cup part-skim Mozzarella cheese, shredded**
1	**can reduced-calorie cream of chicken soup**
1	**can low-sodium cream of mushroom soup**
1/2	**can low-sodium chicken broth**
1	**cup onions, finely diced**
1/2	**cup canned mushrooms**

Nonstick cooking spray

Preheat oven to 350°. Prepare casserole dish by spraying with nonstick cooking spray. Mix cheeses together and set aside.

In a large bowl, mix together both cream soups and chicken broth. Blend well and set aside.

Tear corn tortillas into small pieces. Arrange one layer of tortilla pieces on bottom of prepared casserole dish. Add one half of soup mixture, half of onions, half of mushrooms, one third of cheese and half of chicken. Repeat with remaining ingredients. Top with cheese and bake in 350° oven for one hour. Serve immediately.

Serves 8

Nutrient Analysis: 1 serving
340 Calories, 8.4 g Fat, 2 g Fiber, 672 mg Sodium, 3 g Sat Fat, 62 mg Cholesterol
Diabetic Exchange: 2 BREAD, 1 MILK, 2 MEAT

SWISS ENCHILADAS

Enchiladas Suizas

My dearest friend Ellen gave me this recipe. The tomatillo sauce is high in Vitamin C and is an experience for those who have never tasted it!

1 1/2	**pounds tomatillos, skins removed, cleaned and cut in half**
1/2	**cup cilantro**
2	**teaspoons fresh minced garlic**
1	**teaspoon salt**

Freshly ground pepper

1 1/4	**pounds chicken breast, cooked and shredded**
1	**cup onion, chopped finely (cooked, if desired)**
12	**ounces lowfat Monterey Jack cheese, shredded**
1	**dozen corn tortillas**

Nonstick cooking spray
Lowfat sour cream, optional

Boil tomatillos for five minutes. Tomatillos will be done when they turn a greenish brown color and sink to the bottom of the pan. Drain. Using tongs or fork, add tomatillos to blender or food processor along with garlic and cilantro. Add seasonings, blend until smooth and set aside.

Reserve some cheese for topping the enchiladas. Combine shredded chicken, onion and cheese and set aside.

Preheat oven to 350°.

Prepare tortillas for enchiladas by moistening clean kitchen towel with tap water. Place 2 tortillas in middle of towel and microwave for about 2 minutes or until steamed. Be careful when removing them from oven. Repeat with all tortillas. Tortillas will be steamed and more pliable for filling without breaking. Fill tortillas with a mixture of chicken, onions and cheese. Roll tightly and place seam side down in 9" x 12" pan that has been sprayed with nonstick cooking spray. Repeat with rest of tortillas and filling ingredients.

Cover the enchiladas with tomatillo sauce and sprinkle with a small amount of cheese for garnish. Bake for 20 minutes in a 350° oven.

After serving, garnish with a small amount of imitation sour cream, if desired.

<u>Serves 6</u>

Nutrient Analysis: 1 serving
281 Calories, 6 g Fat, 4 g Fiber, 117 mg Sodium, 2 g Sat Fat, 29 mg Cholesterol
Diabetic Exchange: 2 BREAD, 4 MEAT, 2 VEGETABLE, 1 FAT

WHITE CHILI

Chile Blanco

This chili is lower in cholesterol and saturated fat than regular red chili and tastes great.

1	teaspoon vegetable oil
2	onions, finely chopped
2	cloves minced garlic
2	Serrano chiles, seeded and finely chopped
1	pound white Northern beans, soaked in water overnight
6	cups low-sodium chicken broth, heated
2	tablespoons freshly ground cumin
1	teaspoon oregano
1/4	teaspoon ground cloves
1/2	teaspoon cayenne pepper
4	cups cooked diced chicken breast (1 1/2 pounds)

Salt to taste

Add oil to nonstick skillet. Using medium heat, sauté onions, garlic and Serrano chiles.

Drain beans and add to large crock pot with 6 cups boiling hot chicken broth.

Add onions, garlic and chiles.

Add all seasonings and cook in crock pot at high setting for 6-8 hours. Test for doneness. Add diced chicken and cook for 30 more minutes.

Serves 8

Nutrient Analysis: 1 serving
352 Calories, 4.5 g Fat, 9.5 g Fiber, 68 mg Sodium, 1 g Sat Fat, 65 mg Cholesterol
Diabetic Exchange: 2 1/2 BREAD, 4 MEAT, 1/2 VEGETABLE, 1/2 FAT

POCKET TACOS

Tacos Pita

3/4	**pound ground turkey**
1/4	**pound lean ground beef**
1	**cup onion, chopped finely**
1/2	**teaspoon salt**
1	**garlic clove**
1/3	**teaspoon fresh ground cumin**
1/4	**cup water**
1/4	**cup tomato sauce, no salt added**
4	**ounces lowfat Monterey Jack cheese**

Lettuce, shredded
Tomato, chopped
2   whole wheat pocket (pita) breads, cut in half

Combine ground meats and brown. Drain any excess fat. Add onions and water and cook until tender. Grind garlic and cumin in molcajete. Add 1/4 cup water to loosen spices and add to browned meat. Stir in tomato sauce. Simmer on low heat for about 10 minutes.

Warm pocket bread in toaster or toaster oven, then stuff with ground meat and garnish with lettuce, tomato and lowfat cheese.

Serves 4

Nutrient Analysis: 1 serving
335 Calories, 12 g Fat, 4 g Fiber, 607 mg Sodium, 6 g Sat Fat, 97 mg Cholesterol
Diabetic Exchange: 1 BREAD, 4 MEAT, 1 VEGETABLE, 1/2 FAT

TURKEY BURRITOS

Burritos de Pavo

1   **cup coarsely shredded carrot**
1/4   **teaspoon ground cumin**
1/4   **teaspoon chili powder**
1/4   **cup plain lowfat yogurt**
Juice of one lime
2   **cups cooked turkey breast, shredded**
1/2   **cup tomato, seeded and diced**
Shredded lettuce
1/4   **cup shredded lowfat Cheddar cheese**
8   **corn tortillas**

Combine carrots, cumin, chili powder, yogurt and lime juice in a bowl. Mix thoroughly. Add turkey breast and tomato and toss gently. Warm tortillas on griddle. Divide turkey mixture into eight equal portions and arrange in warmed tortillas. Garnish with lettuce, tomatoes and cheese.

<u>Serves 4</u>

Nutrient Analysis: 1 serving
300 Calories, 7 g Fat, 3 g Fiber, 155 mg Sodium, 2.5 g Sat Fat, 56 mg Cholesterol
Diabetic Exchange: 2 BREAD, 6 MEAT, 1 VEGETABLE, 1 FAT

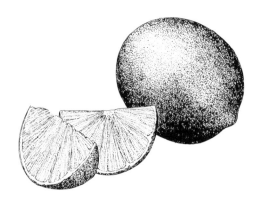

TURKEY CHORIZO

Chorizo de Pavo

Chorizo is used as a spicy breakfast meat, usually prepared in combination with eggs or potatoes and served with tortillas. This recipe tastes great and is a lower-fat replacement for pork chorizo. Some of the turkey may be replaced with very lean ground tenderloin of pork or very lean ground beef.

1	**pound coarsely ground turkey breast**
1	**tablespoon salt**
1	**tablespoon paprika**
1	**tablespoon red chili powder**
1	**clove garlic, finely minced**
2	**tablespoons onions, finely chopped**
1/4	**cup white vinegar**
1/8	**teaspoon oregano**

Mix all ingredients together. Refrigerate overnight to allow flavors to blend.

Brown well before cooking with eggs or diced potatoes.

Serves 8

Nutrient Analysis: 1 serving
49 Calories, 1 g Fat, 1 g Fiber, 833 mg Sodium, tr Sat Fat, 22 mg Cholesterol
Diabetic Exchange: 2 MEAT

TURKEY OLÉ

Pavo Olé

Double recipe

1	pound ground turkey breast, ground without skin
1/2	cup onion, chopped
1	clove garlic, minced
2	teaspoons red chili powder
1/2	teaspoon ground cumin
1/4	teaspoon oregano
1	cup tomato sauce
1/2	cup diced California green chiles, drained
1	cup pinto beans cooked, drained
8	corn tortillas
Shredded lettuce	
4	ounces plain yogurt *Sour Cream Salsa*
1	tomato, seeded and chopped

Add ground turkey to large nonstick frying pan. Add chopped onions and garlic. Sauté using medium heat until turkey has browned. Add spices and tomato sauce and let simmer for about 15 minutes. Add green chiles and pinto beans. Simmer about 15 minutes more.

Warm tortillas on hot griddle.

Arrange turkey mixture on warmed tortillas. Serve with lettuce, tomatoes and yogurt as garnishes.

Serves 4

Nutrient Analysis: 1 serving
361 Calories, 4 g Fat, 8 g Fiber, 955 mg Sodium, tr Sat Fat, 71 mg Cholesterol
Diabetic Exchange: 2 1/2 BREAD, 4 MEAT, 1 1/2 VEGETABLE, 1/2 FAT

TURKEY VERMICELLI

Fideo con Pavo

This is great for using turkey leftovers after the holidays. Children love it, and it's easy to fix.

1   **teaspoon oil**
1 1/2 **cups vermicelli**
1/4   **cup onion, chopped**
1/4   **cup green pepper, chopped**
2   **tablespoons tomato sauce**
2   **cups hot water**
3   **sprigs cilantro, chopped**
2 1/4 **cups cooked turkey, cut in small pieces**

Add oil to a large frying pan and sauté vermicelli over low heat until it turns golden brown, about 10 minutes. Watch vermicelli carefully, as it burns easily.

Add onions and green peppers and sauté about 3 minutes more. Add tomato sauce, water, cilantro and turkey. Bring to a boil. Reduce heat and simmer about 15 minutes uncovered, stirring occasionally until vermicelli is soft.

Serve with beans, a salad and warm tortillas.

<u>Serves 6</u>

Nutrient Analysis: 1 serving
285 Calories, 5 g Fat, 2 g Fiber, 77 mg Sodium,1.5 g Sat Fat, 65 mg Cholesterol
Diabetic Exchange: 2 BREAD, 2 MEAT,

GREEN BURRITOS

Burritos Verdes

1	teaspoon tub margarine
1/2	pound mushrooms, sliced thinly
1/2	green pepper, diced
1	medium tomato, seeded and diced
1	pound lean round steak, excess fat trimmed
1	cup TOMATILLO SAUCE (page 78)
1/2	teaspoon salt
1/2	teaspoon black pepper (or to taste)
8	corn tortillas
4	ounces plain lowfat yogurt

Melt margarine in large nonstick skillet. Sauté mushrooms, green peppers and tomatoes until all are tender. Set aside.

Cut beef into thin strips about 1/4 inch thick. Using same skillet, sauté beef until browned. Combine vegetables with beef strips, then add tomatillo sauce, salt and pepper. Cover and simmer for 20 minutes. Warm tortillas on griddle.

Divide meat and vegetable mixture into the tortillas equally. Top each with yogurt and fasten with a toothpick if necessary. Bake in 350° oven for 5-10 minutes until thoroughly warmed.

Garnish with extra TOMATILLO SAUCE if desired.

Serves 4

Nutrient Analysis: 1 serving
360 Calories, 9 g Fat, 5 g Fiber, 510 mg Sodium, 3 g Sat Fat, 60 mg Cholesterol
Diabetic Exchange: 2 BREAD, 2 VEGETABLE, 4 MEAT, 1/2 FAT

SAUCY BEEF

Carne Guisada

When inviting our military friends over for home-cooked Mexican food, this was one of my favorite recipes. I served it with fresh pinto beans, Mexican rice and freshly cooked corn tortillas—great!

3	**pounds lean round steak, all fat removed, cut into 1" pieces**
1/2	**green pepper, seeded**
3	**large mature tomatoes**
1	**small onion**
3	**cloves garlic**
1/2	**teaspoon red chili powder**
1	**teaspoon salt**
1/2	**teaspoon ground cumin**
1/8	**teaspoon oregano**

Add green pepper, tomatoes, onion, garlic, chili powder and spices to blender or food processor and blend until smooth and puréed. Set aside. Add beef cubes to Dutch oven and brown, draining all excess fat. Combine vegetable purée with beef and bring to a boil. Reduce heat, cover and simmer for 45 minutes.

Serves 8

Nutrient Analysis: 1 serving
265 Calories, 8 g Fat, 1 g Fiber, 402 mg Sodium, 3 g Sat Fat, 92 mg Cholesterol
Diabetic Exchange: 6 MEAT, 1 VEGETABLE

GRILLED LEMON FAJITAS

Fajitas de Limon Parilladas

Barbecues are very popular in Texas, dating back to cowboy days. During the time of cattle drives, meats were cooked on open mesquite fires. Mesquite is a native Texas tree that provides excellent firewood for barbecues, giving meat a wonderful smoked flavor. Mesquite-type briquettes are available for barbecuing fajitas, or you can use real mesquite kindling!

There are many types of marinades we use for fajitas or skirt steak. This marinade is low in fat and easy. Select skirt steak that has been trimmed well and butterflied, if possible.

**1   pound fajitas (skirt steak) trimmed well
        and butterflied
Juice of 4-5 lemons**

Prepare fajitas by removing all excess fat and connective tissue. Add lemon juice and coat well. Put fajitas in airtight container and place in refrigerator. Allow to marinate in refrigerator for 2 days, turning several times.

Cook over very hot mesquite coals for 10-15 minutes on each side.

Serve with rice, beans, PICO DE GALLO and fresh corn tortillas for a real Texas meal!

<u>Serves 4</u>

Nutrient Analysis: 1 serving
165 Calories, 6 g Fat, 0 g Fiber, 86 mg Sodium, 2 g Sat Fat, 64 mg Cholesterol
Diabetic Exchange: 3 MEAT

MEXICAN MEAT AND POTATO STEW

Carne con Papas

1	pound lean round steak, excess fat trimmed, cut into 2" pieces
3	medium potatoes, cubed into 1" pieces, peeled if desired
1/4	cup tomato sauce, no salt added
3	cups water
1	teaspoon salt
3	cloves garlic
1	teaspoon mixed Mexican spices (page 64) ground in molcajete [or 1/2 teaspoon cumin seeds, and 1/4 teaspoon whole black pepper]

In a Dutch oven, brown steak pieces using medium heat. Use no additional oil or fat. Brown until all juices have evaporated. Add cubed potatoes, tomato sauce, water and spices. Bring stew to a boil, then reduce heat and simmer uncovered for about 30 minutes or until potatoes are tender.

Serves 4

Nutrient Analysis: 1 serving
228 Calories, 6 g Fat, 3 g Fiber, 626 mg Sodium, 2 g Sat Fat, 60 mg Cholesterol
Diabetic Exchange: 1 1/2 BREAD, 3 MEAT

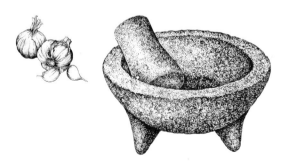

VENISON STEW

Venado Guisado

2	pounds venison
2	tablespoons flour
1	teaspoon oil
6	cups boiling water
Freshly ground pepper	
4	medium potatoes, diced
4	carrots, sliced
4	onions, diced
1/2	teaspoon salt
2	tablespoons flour
Water	

Cut venison in 1" cubes. Roll in flour. Heat oil in nonstick Dutch oven, and sauté venison cubes until well-browned. Add boiling water and pepper to browned meat; cover and simmer 2-3 hours.

Add diced vegetables and cook until tender. Dissolve 2 tablespoons of flour in water and gradually add to stew to thicken.

Serves 8

Nutrient Analysis: 1 serving
250 Calories, 5 g Fat, 4 g Fiber, 252 mg Sodium, 2 g Sat Fat, 65 mg Cholesterol
Diabetic Exchange: 1 BREAD, 3 1/2 MEAT, 2 1/2 VEGETABLE

MASA FOR TAMALES

1/2   **cup softened corn oil tub margarine**
1   **teaspoon salt**
1   **teaspoon baking powder**
2 1/2 **cups Masa Harina (corn flour)**
1 1/8 **cups low-sodium chicken broth, warmed**
2   **tablespoons red chili powder**

Add margarine, salt and baking powder to food processor bowl. Beat until well blended, stopping to scrape sides of bowl.

Add the Masa Harina and blend well.   Add the chicken broth and chili powder and process, stopping occasionally to scrape sides of bowl. Process until ball forms, about one minute.

Refrigerate 2-3 hours or overnight. Cold masa is best for spreading on shucks.

<u>Serves 10</u>

Nutrient Analysis: 1 serving (2 portions tamale masa)
177 Calories, 8 g Fat, tr Fiber, 383 mg Sodium, 2 g Sat Fat, tr Cholesterol
Diabetic Exchange: 1 BREAD, 2 FAT

PREPARING THE SHUCKS

**2   bags dried corn shucks (for order information
        see pages 44-45)**
Warm water
Large container or clean kitchen sink

Fill container or sink with very warm water, and soak the shucks for at least 3 hours.

Carefully remove all corn silk from each shuck and rinse well to remove any debris.

Separate into single layers and set out to prepare for filling. Pat each husk dry to remove excess moisture.

Shucks should be somewhat moist when making tamales. This makes them more pliable and easier to spread.

FILLING THE TAMALES

Fillings of choice
Prepared masa
Prepared shucks
Quart-sized plastic zipper bags or other airtight containers

Prepare a large area to work with tamales. Set out filling(s), masa and shucks. Masa and fillings should be cool. Separate shucks into individual pieces about 8" x 5".

Place one shuck on the palm of your hand. Using the back of a tablespoon, take about 2 tablespoons of masa and spread it evenly on bottom 4 inches of shuck (the larger end). Masa should be thinly spread to allow for even steaming.

Take a small amount of filling and spread on the middle third of the tamale. Carefully roll the tamale from right to left and fold the top part under. Place in plastic bag or container. Using freezer bags, tamales may be frozen for up to 6 months.

STEAMING THE TAMALES

Boiling water

Set a steamer basket in a Dutch oven. Arrange 12 tamales upright in steamer basket, with opening of each tamale facing upward.

Carefully pour boiling water around sides of arranged tamales and quickly cover with aluminum foil and form a seal.

Cover with lid and allow to steam over low heat for 60 minutes.

Open foil seal with caution.

CHICKEN TAMALES

Tamales de Pollo

1   recipe Masa for Tamales (page 169)
Corn shucks

Filling for Tamales
3   half chicken breasts, boiled and shredded
1   teaspoon chili powder
1/2 teaspoon salt
1   large garlic clove
1/2 teaspoon Mexican Spice Mix (or 1/4 teaspoon cumin
     seed and 1/8 teaspoon whole black pepper)
1/2 cup water

Add shredded chicken to large skillet and warm.

Grind garlic and spices in molcajete. Add water to loosen spices and pour into warmed chicken. Add salt and chili powder and stir to blend well.

Warm over medium heat for 10 minutes and set aside.

Prepare shucks with masa. Fill with chicken and roll carefully. Steam in tightly covered Dutch oven for 60 minutes.

Filling is spicy. Decrease spices if desired.

<u>Serves 10</u>

Nutrient Analysis: 1 serving (2 tamales)
221 Calories, 9 g Fat, tr Fiber, 510 mg Sodium, 2 g Sat Fat, 22 mg Cholesterol
Diabetic Exchange: 1 BREAD, 1 MEAT, 2 FAT

VEGETARIAN TAMALES

2   cups pinto beans prepared without bacon (also available canned)

1   recipe Masa for Tamales (page 169)
Corn shucks

Add cooked beans to large saucepan. Using potato masher, mash beans until desired consistency is achieved. Allow beans to simmer gently until most excess liquid has evaporated. Filling should be slightly moist.

Prepare shucks with masa.

Add 1 to 1 1/2 teaspoons beans to prepared shuck and roll carefully.

Steam in tightly covered Dutch oven for 60 minutes.

<u>Serves 10</u>

Nutrient Analysis: 1 serving
221 Calories, 8.4 g Fat, 2.4 g Fiber, 386 mg Sodium, 2 g Sat Fat, tr Cholesterol
Diabetic Exchange: 1 BREAD, 1 MEAT, 2 FAT

ARIZONA-STYLE TAMALES

Tamales Arizona

1   **recipe Masa for tamales (page 169)**
Corn shucks

10   **1-ounce servings string cheese (part-skim Mozzarella)**
20   **strips canned California green chiles, drained**

Spread masa on prepared shucks.

Split each stick of string cheese into 2 equal pieces.

Place one strip of chile and one strip of cheese in each tamale and wrap carefully. Steam in tightly covered Dutch oven for 60 minutes.

Serve immediately.

<u>Serves 10</u>

Nutrient Analysis: 1 serving/2 tamales
253 Calories, 12 g Fat, tr Fiber, 520 mg Sodium, 4.5 g Sat Fat, 16 mg Cholesterol
Diabetic Exchange: 1 BREAD, ! MEAT, 2 1/2 FAT

SIDE DISHES:

VEGETABLES, RICE & BEANS

SIDE DISHES: VEGETABLES, RICE AND BEANS

BROCCOLI MEXICANA

Brocal a la Mejicana

1   pound fresh broccoli
1   cup MORNING SAUCE, warm (page 71)
4   ounces lowfat cheese, finely shredded

Preheat oven to 350°.

Wash broccoli, and cut into stalks, 3-4 inches long. Steam in vegetable steamer for 5 to 6 minutes, or until bright green and tender crisp.

Arrange broccoli in an 9" X 12" baking dish and pour warmed sauce over stems. Sprinkle with shredded cheese. Bake 5-10 minutes in 350° oven, or until cheese melts.

Serve immediately.

<u>Serves 4</u>

Nutrient Analysis: 1 serving
60 Calories, 1 g Fat, 4 g Fiber, 262 mg Sodium, tr Sat Fat, 3 mg Cholesterol
Diabetic Exchange: 1 1/2 VEGETABLE, 1 MEAT

SPICY SQUASH

Calabacitas

1 1/2   teaspoons low-calorie tub margarine
1/2   cup onion, finely chopped
1/2   red pepper, chopped
2   medium zucchini squash, cut in julienne strips
2   yellow squash, cut in julienne strips
1/2   teaspoon salt
1/8   teaspoon chili powder
1   tablespoon cilantro, finely chopped

In a large skillet, melt margarine. Gently sauté onion and red pepper until tender. Add squash and continue to saute about 5 minutes. Just before serving, toss with salt, chili and cilantro.

<u>Serves 6</u>

Nutrient Analysis: 1 serving
65 Calories, 1 g Fat, 4 g Fiber, 193 mg Sodium, tr Sat Fat, 0 mg Cholesterol
Diabetic Exchange: 1 1/2 VEGETABLE, 1/2 BREAD

COLACHE

I found a version of this recipe while browsing through a South American cookbook. It is rich in vitamins and fiber.

1	**pound zucchini, sliced**
1	**cup fresh green beans**
2	**ears fresh corn, quartered**
1/2	**cup chopped onions**
1/2	**cup chopped mushrooms**
3	**fresh tomatoes, quartered and seeded**
1	**cup hominy, drained and rinsed**
1/2	**teaspoon salt**

Nonstick cooking spray

Using vegetable steamer, steam zucchini, green beens and corn quarters for 7 minutes or until tender crisp.

Spray Dutch oven with cooking spray and sauté onions for 5-8 minutes. Add mushrooms and sauté until tender. Add all vegetables and cover, allowing to simmer for about 10 minutes, stirring occasionally. Add salt and serve warm.

<u>Serves 8</u>

Nutrient Analysis: 1 serving
84 Calories, 1 g Fat, 6 g Fiber, 241 mg Sodium, tr Sat Fat, 0 mg Cholesterol
Diabetic Exchange: 1 1/2 VEGETABLE, 1/2 BREAD

GOVERNORS' HOMINY

Posole del Gobernador

While attending the University of Texas at Austin, I worked as a tour guide at the State Capitol and Governors' Mansion. The cooks at the Governors' Mansion were absolutely delightful and shared the original version of this recipe, a favorite of Mrs. Dolph Briscoe.

1	**16-ounce can hominy**
1	**can low-fat mushroom soup**
4	**ounces lowfat cheese, grated (Monterey or Cheddar)**

Heat hominy thoroughly in saucepan. Drain liquid. Add undiluted mushroom soup to hominy and heat thoroughly. Pour into casserole dish.

Add grated cheese. The warm mixture will allow cheese to melt slightly. Serve immediately.

Serves 6

Nutrient Analysis: 1 serving
143 Calories, 2 g Fat, 5 g Fiber, 660 mg Sodium, tr Sat Fat, 5 g Cholesterol
Diabetic Exchange: 1 BREAD, 1 MEAT

GREEN BEAN STEW

Ejotes Guisados

1/2	cup onion, chopped
2	cloves garlic, minced
1	teaspoon oil
1	16-ounce bag frozen green beans
1	16-ounce can tomatoes, no salt added, drained and crushed
1/2	teaspoon salt

Freshly ground pepper

In a large frying pan, sauté onions and garlic in oil until onions are tender. Add frozen green beans, crushed tomatoes, salt and pepper. Simmer 15 minutes, stirring often.

Serves 4

Nutrient Analysis: 1 serving
77 Calories, 1 g Fat, 5 g Fiber, 274 mg Sodium, tr Sat Fat, 0 mg Cholesterol
Diabetic Exchange: 2 VEGETABLE

CHEESY ZUCCHINI

Calabaza con Queso

1/4	cup green onions
1	clove garlic
1	teaspoon oil
6	medium zucchini, sliced thinly
1	16-ounce can corn, drained, no salt added
1/4	cup low-sodium chicken broth
1	tablespoon Parmesan cheese
4	ounces lowfat cream cheese
1/8	teaspoon salt
1/8	teaspoon ground pepper
2	tablespoons 2% milk

In a large nonstick frying pan, heat oil and sauté onions and garlic. Add zucchini and sauté again for about 8 minutes. Mix in corn and toss gently until heated.

Add chicken broth.

Mix together cheeses, salt, pepper, and milk, and blend until smooth. Add to vegetable mixture, warm and serve immediately.

Serves 6

Nutrient Analysis: 1 serving
198 Calories, 5 g Fat, 7 g Fiber, 210 mg Sodium, 1 g Sat Fat, 11 mg Cholesterol
Diabetic Exchange: 2 VEGETABLE, 1 BREAD

MEXICAN CORN

Maiz Mejicano

1/2	cup onion, chopped
1	16-ounce can whole corn, no salt added
2	tablespoons pimentos
1/2	teaspoon oil

In a large nonstick skillet, sauté onions in oil until tender. Add corn and pimentos, and heat thoroughly. Serve warm.

<u>Serves 4</u>

Nutrient Analysis: 1 serving
44 Calories, 1 g Fat, 1 g Fiber, 3 mg Sodium, tr Sat Fat, 0 mg Cholesterol
Diabetic Exchange: 1/2 VEGETABLE, 1 1/2 BREAD

MEXICAN EGGPLANT

Planta de Huevo Mejicano

1 **large eggplant, rinsed and cut crosswise**
2 **cups MORNING SAUCE (page 71)**

In a large skillet with a tight-fitting lid, bring MORNING SAUCE to a boil. Add eggplant and cover tightly. Reduce heat and simmer for 5-7 minutes, or until eggplant is cooked. Serve with extra sauce.

<u>Serves 6</u>

Nutrient Analysis: 1 serving
50 Calories, 1 g Fat, 3 g Fiber, 350 mg Sodium, tr Sat Fat, 0 mg Cholesterol
Diabetic Exchange: 1 1/2 VEGETABLE

MEXICAN HOMINY

Posole Mejicano

1	teaspoon oil
3/4	cup onion, chopped
2 1/2	cups golden hominy, drained
1 1/4	cups canned tomatoes, no salt added, crushed
1	cup nonfat **RED CHILI SAUCE** (see page 73)
4	ounces part-skim Mozzarella cheese, grated

In a large nonstick skillet, sauté onions in oil until tender. Add drained hominy and tomatoes to skillet. Stir to blend together. Add RED CHILI SAUCE and heat thoroughly. Pour into casserole dish and sprinkle with grated cheese. Serve immediately.

Serves 6

Nutrient Analysis: 1 serving
170 Calories, 7.5 g Fat, 6 g Fiber, 330 mg Sodium, 2 g Sat Fat, 11 mg Cholesterol
Diabetic Exchange: 1 VEGETABLE, 1 BREAD, 1 MEAT, 1 FAT

NOPALITO SHAKE

Licuado de Nopalito

In Baja and Southern California, as well as in Southern Texas, many Hispanics believe that the cactus plant has medicinal value in helping diabetes, but this has not been proven. This shake recipe utilizes young cactus leaves and is high in Vitamin C and fiber.

6   ounces prepared orange juice
2   fresh cactus leaves

Blend to liquify. Chill well before drinking.

Serves 1

Nutrient Analysis: 1 serving
180 Calories, 1 g Fat, 8 g Fiber, 14 mg Sodium, 0 gm Sat Fat, 0 mg Cholesterol
Diabetic Exchange: 2 VEGETABLE, 2 1/2 FRUIT

GOLDEN POTATOES

Papitas Doradas

These are favorites with my children. A 2 1/2 ounce serving of regular french fries has about 15 grams of fat and 3 grams of saturated fat. Compare this to only three grams of fat with almost no saturated fat for this recipe!

4   large baking potatoes
1   tablespoon liquid margarine
1/2   teaspoon seasoned salt

Peel and slice potatoes, as if for french fries. On a large cookie sheet, melt margarine in 350° oven.

Place cut potatoes on sheet, and sprinkle lightly with seasoned salt and pepper if desired. Toss with margarine to coat well.

Bake in 350° oven for 45-60 minutes, turning and basting after 30 minutes so that they will brown evenly.

<u>Serves 4</u>

Nutrient Analysis: 1 serving
115 Calories, 3 g Fat, 3 g Fiber, 305 mg Sodium, 1 g Sat Fat, 0 mg Cholesterol
Diabetic Exchange: 2 BREAD, 1/2 FAT

DELICIOUS CABBAGE

Repollo Delicioso

Cabbage is a cruciferous vegetable recommended by the American Cancer Society to aid in the prevention of some types of cancer.

1	**cup onion, chopped**
1	**tablespoon liquid margarine**
1	**head cabbage, washed and cut into eighths**
2	**medium tomatoes, seeded and diced**
1/4	**teaspoon salt**

Freshly ground pepper

In Dutch oven, sauté onions in margarine until tender. Add cabbage, tomatoes and spices. Cover and cook over low heat until cabbage is tender, about 30 minutes.

Serves 8

Nutrient Analysis: 1 serving
60 Calories, 2 g Fat, 5 g Fiber, 117 mg Sodium, tr Sat Fat, 0 mg Cholesterol
Diabetic Exchange: 2 VEGETABLE, 1/2 FAT

SOUTH TEXAS SQUASH CASSEROLE

Calabaza Sur Tejano

Confused about winter and summer squash? Summer squash has a thin peel, easily punctured. A good example would be yellow squash. Winter squash has a hard peel. A Halloween pumpkin is a winter squash.

1	**cup onion, chopped**
1	**teaspoon low-calorie margarine**
7	**cups (about 6) yellow squash, peeled and thinly sliced**
1/2	**cup canned Ro-Tel tomatoes* and green chiles (or similar substitute) crushed**
1/8	**teaspoon freshly ground pepper, or to taste**
4	**ounces part skim Mozzarella cheese, grated**

In a large skillet, melt margarine. Add onions and sauté until they look clear. Add sliced squash and continue to saute 4-5 minutes more, tossing gently.

In a large baking dish (spray with nonstick cooking spray if desired), combine tomatoes, squash and onions. Mix well and add pepper. Sprinkle with grated cheese. Bake 30 minutes in 350°oven, or until bubbly.

Serves 8

Nutrient Analysis: 1 serving
70 Calories, 3 g Fat, 2 g Fiber, 200 mg Sodium, 2 g Sat Fat, 7 mg Cholesterol
Diabetic Exchange: 1 VEGETABLE, 1 BREAD, 1/2 FAT, 1 MEAT

* Ro-Tel tomatoes are a combination of cooked tomatoes and peppers. It is a medium-hot mixture, good with many dishes. Some major tomato companies have similar tomato and pepper products that can be substituted.

SPINACH MEXICAN-STYLE

Espinacas Mejicanas

1   10-ounce package fresh spinach, thoroughly washed
1 1/2   teaspoons extra virgin olive oil
1   small onion, chopped finely
2   garlic cloves, minced
2   tomatoes, seeded and chopped
1/2   teaspoon salt
1/8   teaspoon pepper

In a Dutch oven, heat one quart of water to boiling. Add washed spinach. Bring to a boil, stirring frequently. Reduce heat and simmer about 5 minutes.

With a colander, drain spinach, gently squeezing out water. Set aside. In a large skillet, heat the oil and sauté chopped onion and minced garlic until tender. Add the tomatoes and heat 5 more minutes, stirring fequently. Add drained spinach and heat through. Season with salt and pepper.

Serves 4

Nutrient Analysis: 1 serving
50 Calories, 2 g Fat, 4 g Fiber, 328 mg Sodium, 0 g Sat Fat, 0 mg Cholesterol
Diabetic Exchange: 1 1/2 VEGETABLE, 1/2 FAT

ZUCCHINI

Calabaza

1/2	cup finely chopped onion
1	medium tomato, chopped
1	clove garlic, minced
1	teaspoon oil
6	medium zucchini, sliced horizontally
1	11-ounce can corn, no salt added, drained
1/4	cup lower-sodium chicken broth
4	ounces lowfat cream cheese
4	ounces part-skim Mozzarella cheese, grated
1/8	teaspoon salt
1/8	teaspoon pepper
1/4	cup chopped cilantro, stems removed

In a large skillet with a lid, heat oil and sauté onion, tomatoes and garlic. Add zucchini and corn and warm. Add chicken broth and bring to a boil. Cover and simmer until tender, about 6-8 minutes.

While simmering, cream together the cheeses. Add salt and pepper. Blend together with cooked vegetable mix and add cilantro.

Serve immediately.

Serves 12

Nutrient Analysis: 1 serving
110 Calories, 4 g Fat, 3 g Fiber, 104 mg Sodium, 1.4 g Sat Fat, 11 mg Cholesterol
Diabetic Exchange: 2 VEGETABLE, 1/2 BREAD, 1/2 FAT, 1/2 MEAT

THE BEST MEXICAN RICE

El Arroz Mas Lindo Mejicano

1	cup white rice, uncooked
2	cups hot water
One fresh lemon	
1	teaspoon oil
2	medium tomatoes, seeded and chopped
1/2	medium green pepper, seeded and chopped into small pieces
2	cloves fresh garlic, ground
1	teaspoon cumin, ground
2	cups low-sodium chicken broth
1/4	cup chopped cilantro, or less if desired

In a large bowl, cover rice with hot water. Add juice of one whole lemon, and soak for 5 minutes.

After soaking, drain water using colander. Heat oil in large nonstick skillet. Add well-drained rice and sauté until lightly brown. Stir in tomatoes and green pepper.

Use molcajete to grind garlic and cumin. Use a small amount of water to loosen spices and pour into skillet with rice. Add chicken broth and cilantro, and bring to a boil. Cover, reduce heat and simmer for 20 minutes, or until all liquid is absorbed. Fluff before serving.

<u>Serves 6</u>

Nutrient Analysis: 1 serving
140 Calories, 1 g Fat, 1 g Fiber, 300 mg Sodium, tr Sat Fat, 0 mg Cholesterol
Diabetic Exchange: 1/2 VEGETABLE, 1 1/2 BREAD

BROWN RICE
WITH EPAZOTE

Arroz Integral con Epazote

This is an unusual way to prepare rice. Epazote is an herb used commonly in many foods in Mexico. It adds a unique, nutty taste to foods., and some people say epazote has medicinal qualities. Toasting cumin for this recipe enhances the flavor greatly.

1	**cup brown rice, uncooked**
2 1/2	**cups water**
1/2	**teaspoon salt**
1/2	**cup onion, chopped**
1	**cup fresh tomatoes, diced**
4	**teaspoons fresh epazote, minced**
1/2	**teaspoon cumin seeds, toasted and ground**

In a heavy saucepan with a lid, bring water and salt to a boil. Add brown rice. Bring to a boil again. Cover tightly and simmer on low for 25 minutes. Add vegetables, epazote and cumin. Cover again and simmer for 20 minutes more. Fluff before serving.

<u>Serves 6</u>

Nutrient Analysis: 1 serving
93 Calories, 1 g Fat, 1 g Fiber, 138 mg Sodium, tr Sat Fat, 0 mg Cholesterol
Diabetic Exchange: 1/2 VEGETABLE, 1 1/2 BREAD

CARIBBEAN RICE

Arroz Caribe

A coworker gave me this interesting recipe. Her mother is from Puerto Rico and her father is from Mexico. This recipe blends the two Hispanic cultures. Sazon seasoning can be found in the Hispanic section of grocery stores.

Caribbean Seasoning:

1/4	**cup cilantro**
1/2	**cup onion**
2	**cloves garlic**
1/2	**teaspoon freshly ground cumin**
1	**package Sazon Goya with achiote seasoning**
1/2	**cup water**

Puree all ingredients in blender or food processor until smooth.

1	**teaspoon oil**
2	**cups white rice, uncooked**
1	**tablespoon tomato paste**
3	**tablespoons Caribbean seasoning**
1	**teaspoon salt**
4	**cups water**

Using low to medium heat, sauté rice in oil. Rice will slowly turn a light brown color and must be stirred often to allow for even browning. After rice has browned evenly, add tomato paste, seasoning, salt and water. Stir to blend well. Allow to come to a boil. Reduce heat, cover and simmer for 20 minutes.

<u>Serves 8</u>

Nutrient Analysis: 1 serving
128 Calories, tr Fat, tr Fiber, 103 mg Sodium, tr Sat Fat, 0 mg Cholesterol
Diabetic Exchange: 2 1/2 BREAD

*The sodium content is only an estimate because the sodium content of the Sazon seasoning was unavailable. Caribbean seasoning can be used for other pasta dishes such as vermicelli or with meat. Remainder of seasoning may be kept in refrigerator for about one week or may be frozen in an ice cube tray to use as needed.

COMINO RICE

1	teaspoon oil
1/2	cup onion, chopped
1/2	cup green pepper, chopped
1/4	cup red pepper, chopped
2	garlic cloves, minced or ground in molcajete
1	teaspoon cumin seeds, ground
1	cup brown rice, uncooked
2 1/2	cups low-sodium chicken broth, hot

Heat a large skillet and add oil. Sauté onions and peppers. Add garlic, cumin and rice. Stir until well mixed. Add hot chicken broth. Bring to a boil. Reduce heat, cover and simmer for 45 minutes or until rice is tender. Fluff and serve.

<u>Serves 6</u>

Nutrient Analysis: 1 serving
109 Calories, 2 g Fat, 1 g Fiber, 36 mg Sodium,tr Sat Fat, 1 mg Cholesterol
Diabetic Exchange: 1 BREAD

GREEN RICE

Arroz Verde

1	cup brown rice, uncooked
2 1/2	cups water
1/8	teaspoon salt
1	medium-sized zucchini, grated, about 1 cup
1/4	cup green onions, chopped finely
1/8	cup cilantro, chopped

Bring water to a boil. Add rice and salt. Bring to a boil, cover and reduce heat. Simmer for 45-50 minutes. Add vegetables, cover and steam a few minutes longer.

Fluff before serving.

Serves 6

Nutrient Analysis: 1 serving
127 Calories, 1 g Fat, 2 g Fiber, 275 mg Sodium, 0 g Sat Fat, 0 mg Cholesterol
Diabetic Exchange: 1/2 VEGETABLE, 1 1/2 BREAD

JALAPEÑO RICE

Arroz con Jalapeños

1/2   cup chopped celery
1   tablespoon canned jalapeños, seeded and chopped
1   teaspoon oil
1   cup white rice, uncooked
2   cups lower-sodium chicken broth
1/2   teaspoon cumin, ground

In a large skillet with a lid, sauté celery and jalapeños in oil. Remove from pan.

Add rice and sauté over low heat until rice has turned opaque and slightly brown. Add chicken broth, ground cumin, celery and jalapeños. Bring to a boil and reduce heat. Cover tightly and steam for 20 minutes. Fluff before serving.

Serves 7

Nutrient Analysis: 1 serving
114 Calories, 1 g Fat, 1 g Fiber, 267 mg Sodium, tr Sat Fat, 0 mg Cholesterol
Diabetic Exchange: 1/4 VEGETABLE, 1 1/2 BREAD

LIME RICE

Arroz con Lima

The mother of a patient I worked with in Houston gave me this recipe. It adds a little zip to plain white rice!

2	**cups water**
1	**large clove garlic, minced**

Juice of two limes, divided

1/2	**teaspoon lime peel**
1/4	**teaspoon salt**
1	**cup white rice, uncooked**

Bring water, garlic, lime peel, juice of one lime and salt to boil. Add rice, and allow to come to boil again. Cover tightly, reduce heat and simmer for 20 minutes. Toss gently with remaining lime juice before serving.

Serves 6

Nutrient Analysis: 1 serving
115 Calories, 0 g Fat, 0 g Fiber, 90 mg Sodium, tr Sat Fat, 0 mg Cholesterol
Diabetic Exchange: 1 1/2 BREAD

RICE WITH DRIED SHRIMP

Arroz con Camaron Seco

In South Texas and Northern Mexico, this is a traditional Lenten dish. This version is much lower in fat!

1	**cup white rice, uncooked**
2	**cups water**
1/2	**ounce dried shrimp**
2	**tablespoons diced tomatoes**
1	**teaspoon salt**

Bring water to boil in saucepan with a cover. Add rice, shrimp, tomatoes and salt. Allow to come to boil again. Cover, reduce heat and simmer for 20 minutes.

Fluff before serving.

Serves 6

Nutrient Analysis: 1 serving
120 Calories, tr Fat, tr Fiber, 365 mg Sodium, tr Sat Fat, 8 mg Cholesterol
Diabetic Exchange: 1 1/2 BREAD

SOUTHWESTERN RICE CASSEROLE

Arroz Suroeste

1   **cup brown rice, uncooked**
8   **ounces plain yogurt**
1/2 **cup chopped California green chiles, drained**
4   **ounces Cheddar cheese, grated**
Nonstick cooking spray

Spray casserole dish with nonstick cooking spray.

Cook brown rice as directed on package. Mix rice and yogurt well. Add green chiles. Pour mixture into casserole dish. Sprinkle with grated cheese. Bake in 350° oven for 20 minutes.

<u>Serves 6</u>

Nutrient Analysis: 1 serving
212 Calories, 7 g Fat, 1 g Fiber, 148 mg Sodium, 4 g Sat, 20 mg Cholesterol
Diabetic Exchange: 1 1/2 BREAD, 1 MEAT, 1/4 MILK

TIA'S BEANS

Frijoles de Tia

To test for doneness, blow on a spoonful. If the outer part of the bean "peels" away, they are done!

2	**cups dried pinto beans**
2	**quarts water**
1	**strip bacon**
1 1/2	**teaspoons oil**
2	**carrots, peeled and sliced**
2	**cloves garlic, crushed**

Clean according to package directions. Rinse well with warm water. In a large crock pot, add beans, 2 quarts boiling water, and remaining ingredients. Cover top of crock pot with aluminum foil and top with lid. Cook on high for 4-6 hours, stirring 2-3 times the first hour and then every hour after that. Test beans for doneness after about 4 hours.

One half hour before beans are done add:

5	**dashes Worcestershire sauce**
1	**teaspoon chili powder, more if desired**
1	**medium tomato, diced**
1	**small onion, diced**
1/2	**cup cilantro, chopped**
1/2	**cup chopped green pepper**
1	**teaspoon salt**

Stir gently and continue cooking at high heat in crock pot until beans are done.

<u>Serves 12</u>

Nutrient Analysis: 1 serving
150 Calories, 3 g Fat, 6 g Fiber, 230 mg Sodium, 1 g Sat Fat, 2 mg Cholesterol
Diabetic Exchange: 1/2 VEGETABLE, 2 BREAD, 1/2 FAT

UNFRIED REFRIED BEANS

Frijoles Refritos Sin Freir

To make thick, rich "refried" beans, try the following method. In this version, the taste is still good without the oil or more traditional lard.

3   cups cooked lowfat pinto beans
Nonfat cooking spray

Coat a large nonstick skillet with nonstick cooking spray. Slowly begin to heat cooked beans. Use potato masher and mash beans to desired consistency. Heat for 10-15 minutes or until most excess liquid has evaporated, taking care not to allow beans to become too dry.

<u>Serves 6</u>

Nutrient Analysis: 1 serving
150 Calories, 3 g Fat, 6 g Fiber, 230 mg Sodium, 0 g Sat Fat, 1 mg Cholesterol
Diabetic Exchange: 2 BREAD

DESSERTS

DESSERTS

NOTE

The practice of making flavored teas for use in baked products is common among Mexican cooks. These flavored teas are prepared by boiling a particular spice or herb with water for several minutes to extract the flavor. The "teas" are then incorporated into recipes, imparting their flavor.

Good examples of this are the cinnamon and anise teas I have used in my recipes. Cinnamon tea brewed from cinnamon sticks is wonderful in baked products—but also is delightful as a hot beverage, sweetened with a small amount of honey or sugar. And the aroma is delicious!

When I stayed with my grandmother as a child, there was a tradition to stop housework in the mid-afternoon and enjoy a cup of coffee or cinnamon tea with sweet Mexican pastries.

The thought of *merienda* at my grandmother's evokes memories of the smell of strong coffee being brewed in an aluminum stovetop coffeepot and sweet scents coming from *abuelita's* (grandmother's) bread box.

Merienda was a time to stop and nourish the body, but it was also a time to soothe the spirit and enjoy family or friends. The pace of the day was slowed for time enough to stop and relish the warmth of good food and good company.

On especially cold days, grandmother would prepare hot Mexican chocolate. Milk was gently warmed, and rich chocolate made with Mexican cinnamon was melted into the milk. Cinnamon sticks were added to further enhance the cinnamon flavor. The aroma was beyond compare.

It is with nostalgia that I think of this simpler time we spent "breaking bread" and strengthening family ties.

MANGO SAUCE

Salsa de Mango

Mangoes are rich in Beta Carotene, which has been found to have special properties that may protect against cancer and other illnesses.

1	**mango, peeled and diced**
2	**packets sugar substitute**

Add diced mango along with sugar substitute to blender or food processor. Blend until finely puréed.

Serve over frozen yogurt or non-fat ice cream.

<u>Serves 4</u>

Nutrient Analysis: 1 serving
34 Calories, tr Fat, 1 g Fiber, 1 g Sodium, tr Sat Fat, 0 mg Cholesterol
Diabetic Exchange: 1/2 FRUIT

PINEAPPLE
PAPAYA FREEZE

Helado de Piña y Papaya

This a great, easy nonfat dessert. You can use any fruit nectar to prepare this recipe. There are many wonderful "tropical" nectar blends available at the grocery store.

**2   12-ounce cans pineapple papaya nectar
        (or any tropical nectar blend)**

Freeze nectar in small freezer containers or in ice cube trays. Just before serving, remove from containers by running under warm water. Add to blender and frappé, breaking up ice crystals to make a slush consistency. Serve in dessert glasses.

Serves 4

Nutrient Analysis: 1 serving
100 Calories, 0 g Fat, 0 g Fiber, 0 mg Sodium, 0 g Sat Fat, 0 mg Cholesterol
Diabetic Exchange: 2 FRUIT

FRESH PEACH YOGURT PIE

Pastel de Durazno y Yogur

Make sure to look for whipped topping made without tropical oils.

3 1/4	**cups light whipped topping**
2	**cups yogurt made with sugar substitute, any flavor**
2	**fresh peaches, diced**
1	**ready-made graham cracker crust**

Combine whipped topping and yogurt in large bowl. Place diced peaches on bottom of pie crust. Pour yogurt mixture on top of peaches. Cover tightly and freeze overnight.

<u>Serves 8</u>

Nutrient Analysis: 1 serving
196 Calories, 9 g Fat, tr Fiber, 155 mg Sodium, 0 g Sat Fat, 1.5 mg Cholesterol
Diabetic Exchange: 1 FRUIT, 1 FAT, 1/2 MILK

PIÑA COLADA PIE

Pastel de Piña Colada

This is an easy dessert, lower in calories, but it may have some tropical oils and saturated fats, depending on ingredients. Use it for a special occasion.

3 1/4	cups light whipped topping
16	ounces piña colada yogurt
1	cup crushed pineapple, drained well
1	ready-made graham cracker pie crust

In a large mixing bowl, mix together whipped topping, yogurt and pineapple. Add to crust. Cover tightly. Freeze overnight.

Serves 8

Nutrient Analysis: 1 serving
243 Calories, 12 g Fat, tr Fiber, 155 mg Sodium, 0 g Sat Fat, 2.5 mg Cholesterol
Diabetic Exchange: 1 BREAD, 1 FRUIT, 2 FAT

MARINATED FRUIT DESSERT

Postre de Fruta

This is a good fruit salad for brunch or as a lovely dessert. This recipe does have a significant amount of sugar, so diabetics should consume only small amounts as part of a healthy eating plan.

1/2	cup sugar
1	cup water
1/2	teaspoon lemon juice
1/2	cup kirsch liqueur
2	cinnamon sticks, broken
1/2	teaspoon whole allspice
1/2	teaspoon whole cloves
3	large apples, cut in chunks
3	large navel oranges, peeled and cut in chunks
1	small pineapple, cut in chunks
1	small cantaloupe, cut in chunks
1	pint fresh strawberries, sliced

Combine sugar, water, lemon juice and liqueur in saucepan. Tie cinnamon, allspice and cloves in a cheesecloth "ball". Add to marinade. Bring to a boil, reduce heat and simmer on low heat for 5 minutes. Let cool. Remove spices.

Place all fruits except strawberries in a large bowl. Pour cooled marinade over fruits. Toss gently. Refrigerate 5-6 hours or overnight. Just before serving, stir in strawberries. Serve in dessert glasses.

<u>Serves 10</u>

Nutrient Analysis: 1 serving
170 Calories, 1 g Fat, 4 g Fiber, 7 mg Sodium, tr Sat Fat, 0 mg Cholesterol
Diabetic Exchange: 2 FRUIT

PEARS IN STRAWBERRY SAUCE

Peras con Purée de Fresa

1	**14-ounce can pears, canned in own syrup**
12	**fresh strawberries**
3	**packages sugar substitute**

Nondairy whipped topping, optional

Drain pears. Cut into 1" cubes and set aside.

In a food processor or blender, puree strawberries and sugar substitute until smooth.

Layer pear chunks and strawberry sauce in dessert glasses. Garnish with a small amount of nondairy whipped topping, if desired.

Serves 4

Nutrient Analysis: 1 serving
75 Calories, 0 g Fat, 3 g Fiber, 5 mg Sodium, 0 g Sat Fat, 0 mg Cholesterol
Diabetic Exchange: 1 FRUIT

SUMMER DELIGHT

Fruta de Verano

1	**cup sliced strawberries**
3	**teaspoons sugar or equivalent amount of sugar substitute**
1	**tablespoon lime juice**
1	**large cantaloupe**
1	**cup green or red seedless grapes**

Purée strawberries, sugar and lime juice in blender or small processor. Cut cantaloupe into small chunks. Toss grapes and cantaloupe with strawberry sauce. Cover and refrigerate 2 hours.

Spoon fruit into dessert glasses.

Serves 4

Nutrient Analysis: 1 serving
84 Calories, 0 g Fat, 2 g Fiber, 12 mg Sodium, 0 g Sat Fat, 0 mg Cholesterol
Diabetic Exchange: 1 FRUIT

FRUIT IN AMARETTO CREAM

Fruta en Crema de Amaretto

This is one of my favorite desserts when I entertain. It is healthy and delicious.

1 1/2	**tablespoons Amaretto liqueur***
3	**packages sugar substitute or 2 tablespoons brown sugar (or to taste)**
1	**cup vanilla-flavored yogurt (sweetened with sugar substitute)**
5	**cups fresh, sliced strawberries or mangos or any mix of fresh fruit**
2	**tablespoon slivered almonds, toasted**

Combine liqueur, sugar and yogurt, making a cream. Stir long enough to dissolve all sugar. Place fruit in dessert glasses. Add Amaretto cream to top of fruits. Garnish with slivered almonds.

Serves 4

Nutrient Analysis: 1 serving
118 Calories, 3 g Fat, 2 g Fiber, 46 mg Sodium, tr Sat Fat, 1 mg Cholesterol
Diabetic Exchange: 1 FRUIT, 1/4 MILK, 1 FAT

* Almond extract may also be used to flavor yogurt.

MANGOS AND CREAM

Mangos con Crema

This recipe is very high in both Vitamin A and Vitamin C. Both fruits contribute to its nutritional value.

1	**cup lowfat vanilla yogurt**
3	**teaspoons brown sugar (or to taste)**
2	**teaspoons almond extract**
2	**large mangos**
4	**large strawberries**
1/4	**cup slivered almonds, toasted**

Mint leaves (optional)

Beat yogurt, sugar and almond extract together until smooth. Divide evenly into four dessert plates.

Peel mangos and slice into about 16 slices. Arrange in a sunburst pattern on each plate.

In a blender or mini-processor, purée strawberries. Pour strawberry sauce in center of mangos.

Garnish with toasted almonds or mint leaves.

<u>Serves 4</u>

Nutrient Analysis: 1 serving
142 Calories, 3 g Fat, 2.6 g Fiber, 46 mg Sodium, tr Sat Fat, 1 mg Cholesterol
Diabetic Exchange: 1 1/2 FRUIT, 1/4 MILK, 1 FAT

FRESH PAPAYA

Papaya Fresca

1   **papaya, fresh**
8   **ounces frozen raspberry yogurt, softened**
1/2   **cup frozen raspberries**
2   **packages sugar substitute**

Halve the papaya. Scoop out seeds and discard. Fill the cavity with softened raspberry yogurt. Return papaya to freezer and freeze overnight. In mini-processor or blender, puree raspberries with sugar substitute. Strain to remove seeds, if desired. Save puree in container until ready to serve.

Just before serving, remove papaya from freezer. Peel skin and place on dessert dish. Drizzle with raspberry sauce. Serve immediately.

Serves 2

Nutrient Analysis: 1 serving
170 Calories, 0 g Fat, 5 g Fiber, 65 mg Sodium, 0 g Sat Fat, 3 mg Cholesterol
Diabetic Exchange: 2 FRUIT, 1/2 MILK

STRAWBERRIES IN CINNAMON SAUCE

Fresas en Salsa Canela

This dessert is a great source of Vitamin C and easy to make.

1	**cup lowfat vanilla yogurt**
1	**teaspoon cinnamon**
2	**teaspoons sugar (or to taste) or equivalent amount of sugar substitute**
5	**cups strawberries, washed and hulled**

About 2 hours before serving, prepare the sauce by blending yogurt, cinnamon and sugar. Blend until sugar completely dissolves.

Immediately before serving, slice strawberries into 4 dessert glasses. Spoon cinnamon sauce over strawberries.

Serve chilled.

<u>Serves 4</u>

Nutrient Analysis: 1 serving
120 Calories, 1.5 g Fat, 4 g Fiber, 39 mg Sodium, .5 g Sat Fat, 2.7 mg Cholesterol
Diabetic Exchange: 1 FRUIT, 1/4 MILK

MANGO MOLD

Gelatina de Mango

2	packages sugar-free orange-flavored gelatin
1	package sugar-free lemon-flavored gelatin
1	cup boiling water
8	ounces lowfat cream cheese
1	cup fresh mango, diced

Add gelatins and boiling water to blender container. Cover and blend until powder dissolves. Add cream cheese and mango pieces to blender and process all ingredients until smooth. Pour into mold or other container. Refrigerate until set.

Garnish with mango slices if desired.

Serves 8

Nutrient Analysis: 1 serving
55 Calories, 1 g Fat, .5 g Fiber, 185 mg Sodium, 0 g Sat Fat, 0 mg Cholesterol
Diabetic Exchange: 1/4 FRUIT

TROPICAL FRUIT MOLD

Gelatina Tropical

If you've got a sweet tooth, this is a great low-calorie, low-sugar dessert. It is good enough for company!

2	**packages sugar-free orange gelatin**
2	**cups boiling water**
12	**ounces guava nectar**
1	**mango, peeled and cut in small cubes**

Dissolve orange gelatin in 2 cups boiling water. Add cold guava nectar and blend well. Pour into dessert glasses. Refrigerate until slightly thickened. Add mango cubes. Refrigerate until firm. Serve cold.

Serves 8

Nutrient Analysis: 1 serving
52 Calories, 0 g Fat, 5 g Fiber, 50 mg Sodium, 0 mg Sat Fat, 0 mg Cholesterol
Diabetic Exchange: 1 FRUIT

KAHLUA PARFAIT

Pudin de Kahlua

Kahlua is a coffee-flavored liqueur that is produced in Mexico.

1	**package sugar-free chocolate pudding**
2	**cups minus 1 tablespoon skim milk**
1	**tablespoon Kahlua**
1/2	**cup frozen raspberries**
1/2	**cup light whipped topping, optional***

Prepare pudding with milk and Kahlua. Fill glasses with pudding and top with whipped topping if desired. Refrigerate. Top with slightly thawed raspberries before serving.

Serves 4

Nutrient Analysis: 1 serving
126 Calories, tr Fat, 2 g Fiber, 330 mg Sodium, tr Sat Fat, 0 mg Cholesterol
Diabetic Exchange: 1/2 BREAD, 1/4 FRUIT, 1/2 MILK

* Whipped topping should be used only occasionally. Most are prepared with tropical oils.

RICE PUDDING

Atole de Arroz

This is a lower-calorie, lower-fat version of that wonderful, warm pudding my mom used to make on chilly winter nights.

1/3	**cup evaporated skim milk**
1/2	**cup brown sugar**
2	**cups white rice, cooked, warm**
1/3	**cup raisins, simmered in cinnamon tea***
1/2	**teaspoon vanilla**
1/4	**teaspoon ground cinnamon**

Add milk and brown sugar to saucepan and simmer gently until sugar has dissolved. Add rice, raisins, vanilla and cinnamon. Stir to blend all ingredients.

Pour warm pudding into dessert glasses.

Serve warm or cold.

<u>Serves 4</u>

Nutrient Analysis: 1 serving
233 Calories, 0 g Fat, 1 g Fiber, 31 mg Sodium,0 g Sat Fat, 1 mg Cholesterol
Diabetic Exchange: 1/2 FRUIT, 1 BREAD (does contain sugar)

* Cinnamon tea is prepared by breaking one or two fresh cinnamon sticks in half and adding 2-3 cups water to a saucepan. Bring this mixture to a rapid boil. Boil 15-20 minutes. Strain to remove cinnamon sticks. Adding raisins to the cinnamon tea will make them plump and flavorful.

BANANAS
IN CINNAMON SAUCE

Platanos con Canela

This dessert is easy to make, and the ingredients are usually on hand.

4	**bananas, firm**
1/4	**cup granulated sugar**
1/2	**teaspoon cinnamon**
4	**teaspoons tub margarine**

Low-calorie whipped topping, optional

Preheat oven to 325°.

Peel bananas. Slice in half and then slice each half vertically. Combine sugar, cinnamon and margarine in microwave dish. Microwave for approximately 30 seconds to melt margarine. Stir well to blend. Pour syrup over bananas.

Bake bananas in ovenproof dish for 15 minutes at 325°.

Baste frequently with sauce.

Serve warm garnished with whipped topping, if desired.

<u>Serves 4</u>

Nutrient Analysis: 1 serving
180 Calories, 3 g Fat, 2 g Fiber, 48 mg Sodium, 1.5 g Sat Fat, 0 mg Cholesterol
Diabetic Exchange: 2 FRUIT, 1 FAT

MANGO FLAN

Flan de Mango

The cholesterol and fat contents in this version of a favorite Mexican dessert, flan, are much lower than the original.

1 1/2	**cups sugar, divided**
1	**cup egg substitute**
2	**cups skim milk**
1/2	**teaspoon almond extract**
1	**4-ounce jar mango dessert baby food**

Preheat oven to 250° and prepare 6 custard cups for flan.

Add one cup of sugar to large nonstick skillet. Over medium heat, begin to caramelize sugar. Stir often, watching carefully to prevent sugar from scorching. Sugar will liquefy and turn an amber brown color. This process takes about 5-6 minutes. If sugar begins to smoke it has cooked too long or has been overheated, and this step will have to be repeated. Immediately after sugar caramelizes, divide evenly into custard cups. Caramelized sugar will harden fast.

In a large mixing bowl, mix together remaining sugar, egg substitute, milk, extract and mango dessert together until well blended. Divide evenly into custard cups.

Set custard cups in 9 x 12 baking pan containing 1 inch of hot water. Bake in this water bath for 1 1/2 to 2 hours or until knife inserted in center comes out clean. Allow to cool in refrigerator 5-6 hours or overnight. To serve, run a knife around custard cup edges and invert on dessert plate. Garnish with fresh berries, toasted almonds or strips of fresh mango, if desired.

<u>Serves 6</u>

Nutrient Analysis: 1 serving
315 Calories, 6 g Fat, 0 g Fiber, 121 mg Sodium, tr Sat Fat, 7 mg Cholesterol
Diabetic Exchange: 1 MEAT, 1/2 FRUIT, 1/2 MILK

BAKED APPLES

Manzanitas

4   tart apples (Granny Smith)
1/4   cup brown sugar
1   tablespoon tub margarine
4   cinnamon sticks
Low-calorie whipped topping, optional

Preheat oven to 350°. Wash and core apples, but do not cut entirely through apple. Leave a small amount of flesh and skin on the bottom of the apple. In a medium sized baking dish lined with foil, place cored apples, and fill each apple hole with one tablespoon brown sugar. Divide margarine into 4 pieces and add one piece to each apple. Add cinnamon stick. Bake in 350° oven for 30-40 minutes, or until apples are tender. Remove cinnamon sticks before eating.

Serve with low-calorie whipped topping, if desired.

<u>Serves 4</u>

Nutrient Analysis: 1 serving
145 Calories, 2 g Fat, 4 g Fiber, 40 mg Sodium, 0 g Sat Fat, 0 mg Cholesterol
Diabetic Exchange: 1 FRUIT, 1/2 FAT

FRESH APPLE TARTS

Empanadas de Manzana Fresca

2	tart cooking apples (Granny Smith)
1/2	teaspoon cinnamon
2	packets sugar substitute
4	slices bread

Nonstick cooking spray
Sandwich toaster

Peel, core and dice apples. Add to nonstick saucepan and toss with cinnamon. Cook over medium-low heat, stirring frequently, until apples have become soft, about 20 minutes. When apples have softened, add sugar substitute. Toss gently. Spray sandwich maker with nonstick cooking spray. Add one slice of bread and one half of the cooked apples. Cover with second slice of bread and bake until golden brown, about 3 minutes.

Repeat procedure with other ingredients.

Serve warm.

<u>Serves 4</u>

Nutrient Analysis: 1 serving
104 Calories, 1 g Fat, 2 g Fiber, 126 mg Sodium, tr Sat Fat, tr Cholesterol
Diabetic Exchange: 1 BREAD, 1 FRUIT

MANGO FRUIT CRUNCH

Postre de Mango

This recipe is easy and can be adapted to include any combination of fruits on hand. It is much lower in saturated fat than the original recipe.

3/4	**cup rolled oats**
1/2	**cup brown sugar**
1/3	**cup flour**
1/2	**teaspoon ground cinnamon**

Dash salt

3	**tablespoons oil**
3	**large tart apples (Granny Smith), peeled and diced**
1	**mango, diced**

Yogurt, frozen yogurt or nonfat ice cream, optional

Preheat oven to 350°.

Combine rolled oats, brown sugar, flour, cinnamon, salt and oil in a mixing bowl. Mix until all ingredients have blended well.

Add diced apples and mango to pie pan. Cover with oat mix.

Bake in 350° oven for about 30 minutes.

Serve with yogurt, frozen yogurt or nonfat ice cream.

<u>Serves 8</u>

Nutrient Analysis: 1 serving
188 Calories, 6 g Fat, 2.7 g Fiber, 42 mg Sodium, tr Sat Fat, 0 mg Cholesterol
Diabetic Exchange: 1/2 BREAD, 1 FRUIT, 1 FAT

MEXICAN FRUIT BETTY

Postre de Fruta Betty

3   tablespoons sugar
1/2   stick cinnamon
3   cups fresh peaches, washed and sliced
Juice of one fresh lime
1/4   cup brown sugar
1   tablespoon oil
1/2   cup flour

Preheat oven to 375°.

Add white sugar and cinnamon stick to blender container. Blend until cinnamon stick has been completely mixed into sugar. This will take about 5 minutes. Stop and start the blender to assure all parts of the stick have been completely pulverized.

Add fresh fruit to pie pan and toss gently with the lime juice. Add the sugar-cinnamon mixture and toss again.

Bake in 375° oven for about 45 minutes.

While fruit is baking, combine brown sugar, oil and flour using a fork, until mixture is crumbly. After 45 minutes, place this mixture on top of the baked fruit and return to oven for about 15 minutes, or until top is brown.

<u>Serves 4</u>

Nutrient Analysis: 1 serving
290 Calories, 4 g Fat, 3 g Fiber, 5 mg Sodium, .5 g Sat Fat, 0 mg Cholesterol
Diabetic Exchange: 2 1/2 FRUIT, 1 BREAD, 1 FAT

LITTLE GIFTS

Regalitos

The idea for this dessert came from a Mexican restaurant we enjoyed in Houston. While their version had a similar filling in a deep-fried pastry, my version is much lower in fat and calories.

1/2	cup seedless raisins
1/4	cup granulated sugar
1 1/2	cups water
2	tablespoons cornstarch
1/4	teaspoon cinnamon
2	firm bananas, sliced vertically
2	sheets phyllo dough
2	teaspoons liquid margarine

Preheat oven to 350°.

Defrost phyllo dough according to package directions.

Add raisins, sugar and water to a medium-sized sauce pan. Bring to a boil. Reduce heat. Use 2 tablespoons water to make cornstarch a smooth paste and slowly add to raisins and water. Stir until thickened. Add cinnamon and bananas. Stir until well blended. Keep warm.

Brush each phyllo layer with margarine and cut into quarters. Add fruit mixture to the center of each of the four quarters. Bring up corners and bunch together around fruit mixture to form "bundle". Bake in 350° oven for 10 minutes or until golden brown. Serve warm.

Serves 4

Nutrient Analysis: 1 serving
200 Calories, 3 g Fat, 2 g Fiber, 88 mg Sodium, .5 g Sat Fat, 0 mg Cholesterol
Diabetic Exchange: 1/2 BREAD, 2 FRUIT, 1/2 FAT

OIL PASTRY FOR PUMPKIN EMPANADAS AND COYOTITAS

Pan Para Empanadas y Coyotitas

4	tablespoons sugar
1	teaspoon cinnamon
2	cups sifted cake flour
1/2	cup oil
2 to 3 tablespoons iced cinnamon tea*	

Preheat oven to 350°.

Sift together sugar, cinnamon and flour. Using pastry blender, add oil and blend until mixture becomes crumbly. Sprinkle iced cinnamon tea, 1 tablespoon at a time and gather dough together. Knead for 3 to 5 minutes and form into a ball. Refrigerate for at least one hour. Remove from refrigerator and form 12 equal sized balls.

Using rolling pin, roll out dough into 5 to 6 inch circles, about 1/16" thick.

Fill with desired filling and dust lightly with mixture of:

1/4	cup sugar
1	teaspoon cinnamon

* Cinnamon tea is made by boiling cinnamon sticks with water for about 15-20 minutes. Cool before using in pastry recipe.

PUMPKIN EMPANADAS

Empanadas de Calabaza

1   recipe OIL PASTRY (see page 230)

3/4   cup canned pumpkin
1 1/2   tablespoons sugar
1   teaspoon cinnamon
Nonstick cooking spray

TOPPING
1/4   cup sugar
1   teaspoon cinnamon

In a small mixing bowl, mix together pumpkin, sugar and cinnamon. Set aside. Prepare topping in separate bowl. Set aside.

Preheat oven to 350°. Roll out pastry dough into 5-inch circles. Add one teaspoon mixture to middle section of circle.

Fold over circle to form semi-circle. Pinch together edges to form a tight seal. Pierce top layer to allow steam to escape.

Sprinkle Empanadas lightly with topping.

Prepare a cookie sheet by spraying with nonstick cooking spray. Place Empanadas on cookie sheet and bake for 25 minutes or until light brown.

Serves 12

Nutrient Analysis: 1 serving
195 Calories, 9 g Fat, 1 g Fiber, 1 mg Sodium, 0 g Sat Fat, 0 mg Cholesterol
Diabetic Exchange: 1 BREAD, 2 FAT

COYOTITAS

1   recipe OIL PASTRY (page 230)

3   large cooking apples (Granny Smith),
        peeled and chopped finely
Juice of 2 large limes
4   tablespoons sugar
Nonstick cooking spray

TOPPING
1/4   cup sugar
1   teaspoon cinnamon

Preheat oven to 350°.

Roll out pastry dough into 5-inch circles.

Toss chopped apples with lime juice and sugar. Cover and set aside. Add 1-2 teaspoons apple mixture to middle section of circle.

Fold over circle to form semi-circle. Pinch together edges to form a tight seal. Pierce top layer to allow steam to escape.

Sprinkle lightly with cinnamon/sugar mixture.

Prepare a cookie sheet by spraying lightly with nonstick cooking spray. Place Coyotitas on cookie sheet and bake for 25 minutes, or until light brown.

<u>Serves 12</u>

Nutrient Analysis: 1 serving
205 Calories, 9 g Fat, 1 g Fiber, 1 mg Sodium, 0 g Sat Fat, 0 mg Cholesterol
Diabetic Exchange: 1 BREAD, 1/2 FRUIT, 1 FAT

STRAWBERRY BANANA PARFAIT

Pudin de Fresa y Platano

1	**package sugar-free banana pudding**
2	**cups skim milk**
14	**strawberries**
3	**packages sugar substitute**

Prepare banana pudding using skim milk.

In a food processor or blender, blend 8 strawberries until smooth. Add sugar substitute and blend again.

Layer prepared pudding and strawberry sauce in dessert glasses.

Garnish with fresh strawberries anchored on glasses.

Serves 6

Nutrient Analysis: 1 serving
96 Calories, tr Fat, 2 g Fiber, 330 mg Sodium, 0 g Sat Fat, 0 mg Cholesterol
Diabetic Exchange: 1/2 STARCH, 1/4 FRUIT, 1/2 MILK

PIÑA COLADA PUDDING

Pudin de Piña Colada

1   **package vanilla sugar-free pudding**
2   **cups skim milk**
1   **teaspoon coconut extract**
1   **cup crushed pineapple, well drained**
Maraschino cherries, optional

Prepare pudding according to package directions. Add coconut extract. Fold in well drained crushed pineapple. Pour into dessert glasses and garnish with cherry, if desired.

Serves 4

Nutrient Analysis: 1 serving
125 Calories, tr Fat, 1.5 g Fiber, 330 mg Sodium, 0 g Sat Fat, 0 mg Cholesterol
Diabetic Exchange: 1/2 STARCH, 1/2 FRUIT, 1/2 MILK

INDEX

Whole Wheat

Yogurt

Recipes were analyzed using:

Sante (For Good Health) Hopkins Technology. Hopkins, Minnesota, 1991.

Nutritionist III. N-Squared Computing. Salem, Oregon. 1989

Appletree Press Title Order Form

HEALTHY MEXICAN COOKING: Authentic Low-Fat Recipes. Delicious, traditional Mexican foods with few ingredients, practical preparations and moderate to low calories. Plus, glossary, special mail-order section and more than 160 wonderful, authentic recipes! 256 pages, Softcover with lie-flat binding. Available in English or Spanish editions. *$15.95 each...Send me____for a total of $_____*

THE ESSENTIAL ARTHRITIS COOKBOOK: Kitchen Basics for People with Arthritis, Fibromyalgia and Other Chronic Pain and Fatigue. Excellent nutrition information, medication tables, photos and illustrations, overcoming energy-robbers, when eating is difficult, useful resources and tools, 120 low-fat recipes that save time and energy! 288 pages, Hardcover with Double-wire O binding for ease in the kitchen. *$24.95 each...Send me____for a total of $_____*

COOKING ALA HEART The Classic! With more than 92,000 copies in print, its recipes are always hailed as original, delicious and easy to make. Selected by the editors of the Harvard Medical School health letters, this book features two chapters of sound nutrition information and over 400 recipes! 456 pages, Softcover with lie-flat binding. *$19.95 each...Send me____for a total of $_____*

WHAT'S FOR BREAKFAST? The easiest way to stop cheating yourself of a good breakfast! Over 100 delicious and easy recipes divided by preparation time: Super Quick, Quick and Worth the Effort — all low in fat and calories. The "Pro-Carb" Connection to hold off hunger, special shopping sections and menus for all occasions! 264 pages, Softcover with lie-flat binding. *$13.95 each...Send me____for a total of $_____*

SHIPPING
Add $4.00 for one book, $5.00/2 books, $6.00/3 books, $7.00/4-6 books.......*total $_____*

Minnesota residents...Add 6.5% sales tax $_____

TOTAL ENCLOSED $_____

Circle one: Check   Visa   MasterCard

Card #_____Exp. Date_____

Ship to: _____

Street address_____

City, State and Zip Code_____

Mail your order to:
Appletree Press Inc.   Suite 125   151 Good Counsel Drive   Mankato, MN 56001
or Order Toll Free #800-322-5679